Don't Miss the Internet Tide

"A Rising Tide Lifts All Boats"

The days the cost of starting a business was prohibitive are gone and anyone can start a profitable business on the Internet. The catch, however, is there is a way to go about doing it. Because wasting time and resources on the outset scouring for the right information could go a long way and that is what this publication alleviates. It will save you time by availing you all the basics you will need to run an effective business online and would enable you to focus on running your business. If you are already running an online business there might be a few strategies you have overlooked and it could be affecting your business if it is not profitable. So, why not revamp your existing strategies with some of the tested and proven methods outlined in the book.

You are always welcome to send your comments to
optinpromo@mailas.com

Don Trevor

2007

ISBN 978-1-4303-1959-7

PREFACE

There is no denying that WWW is still a new medium most people are trying to get familiar with. Among them, there are a few who would want to use it to do a profitable business. The good news is it is possible to start a profitable venture of many kinds on the Internet. If there is a catch, the would be entrepreneurs would have to know what it takes to start and promote a business online, because that is what will make or break a business. Since it is a new medium the technology is totally different and it is evolving as we write here. This means it is possible to get the basics through publications such as this, but it would up to the entrepreneurs to do the necessary follow up not to fall behind in their pursuit to start a profitable business on the Internet.

The main reason why this book came into existence is the particular information that will enable webmasters do an effective business is scattered all over the place on the Internet, and it takes a while to come across all of it. But when that part of the job is done by someone who had been tracking the Internet business for a long time, even if making the venture successful depends on what the webmasters do if they get some help to save them time and to give them edge, they would definitely be benefited. Based on such analysis the basics of what it would mean to start an online business is discussed here. And anyone who is starting out or had been around for a while and has hit a snag because of not doing the right things will immensely be benefited from the material that had been put together for the convenience of would be webmasters in this booklet.

CONTENTS

Marketing Strategy

Marketing Strategy for Starting an Internet Business

Making money on the Internet is possible and there are a good number of people who are succeeding even if there is enough proof that it is a totally new medium that requires a totally different approach. This should not be a surprise to anyone because, the same thing happens in the real world. No two kinds of line of works are the same, needles to mention categories here, because most definitely they will have some common denominators, but for the most part each one of them require a different approach. The client base might be the same and the business might require a gearing toward a certain sector of the market.

A business selling auto parts cannot expect those who are riding their bike or those who are using public transport to be its targeted customers. Those sectors first will have to change their status and start using a vehicle like a car to become prospects, and that job is, more or less, out of the hand of the auto part seller per se and it is the job of the car dealerships to convert as many pedestrians as possible to become car owners. However, it is possible that the auto part seller could be chipping in indirectly or even directly in the campaign of converting pedestrians into car owners. He can do the promotion for a fee or free, as part of a long-term plan, to raise the client base of those who are dependent on cars for generating income. It could also be a concerted effort across the board so that the aggregate business will benefit from a high number of car owners.

The same thing is applicable when one thinks about making money on the Internet, in such a way that, since it is becoming very huge, it is very difficult to be certain which entry-point will be the most profit generator. Like the offline business, the online business will have to go through the right preparation phase in order to be an effective money-generating vehicle. Obviously, it has its own advantages and it would not be held in high regard if it does not hold a promise, to say the least, or an immediate result if it is executed using tested procedures.

First, there has to be some product or service that will have to come to the marketplace, which is basic. One can start out with a hobby site and contemplate to generate money from it. However, the key here is, like any offline business, sellers will have to come up with a product that sells. Once that stage is surpassed then what follows is charting what to do next to put that product on the hand of interested buyers. Because, interested buyers like to scour the Internet searching for what they are looking for, whatever it might be. At the same time sellers who know what is in demand in the marketplace are out there with those products and services.

The similarity ends here and the arduous role of becoming a seller kicks in. There are many sellers as there are many buyers and what buyers are looking at is the price ratio compared to the value they are getting from the product they are buying. If they see a good coloration between the two, they are always willing to part with their money. The sellers also know what the buyers want. They want good products and services that will render the required values by paying reasonably. The question that pops up in their mind is whether that reasonable price is profitable, because unless they make profit that is unless they cover their cost and be rewarded somehow for their effort, it is not worth to be engaged in the business, since it does not make economic sense. They can afford to charge so much low price before they throw the towel.

Nevertheless, for the buyers, because of the prevalent competition, all they have to do is hunt for bargains, and they will buy the particular products they are looking for when they reason that the price is sensible. Consequently, the same psychology is applicable on the Internet too. The exception is the new medium is found to be facilitating the traditional trade in such a way that, because it is inexpensive compared to keeping and moving physical goods like the brick-and-mortar setup, buyers will be highly benefited as what they pay is the accrual cost the sellers incur for the most part. Yet, there are certain goods that are more suitable for the Internet more than others are that could easily get ahead a notch from regular goods that we will touch on as we churn forward. One thing certain is, it is possible to sell almost anything on the Internet. In fact, sellers could get a much wider market because of the simplicity of availing their products and services on the Internet for a big number of buyers to browse through. Such a process presumably makes the order easy, whether they made it from their home or workplace, and the product they ordered could easily find its way to the shipping address they provided.

There will, of course, be advantages and disadvantages, likes and dislikes, like where for example if a buyer goes out and buys a product from a store, he or she can have the product in their possession immediately instead of waiting for it to arrive in the mail. At times it is much better to touch and feel the products bought than waiting to do so, after paying for it. After waiting for several weeks, if the buyer does not like what has arrived through the delivery system it can be returned, and the time involved, or the extra expense that the buyer has to incur might not make it worthwhile. However, there are detractors as well as advantages too; also all goods might not be the same. The time one will save might be considerable, where for example instead of going shopping after a long day at work, one can do the purchasing within a few minutes on a lunch break, and know for sure the item will be delivered on time.

No matter, as in everything else, the consumer hat its own choice, and the advantages are taking over the detractors and doing business on the Internet has not become only chic, but essential too. It is proven that studying the products that customers are buying without being rushed or hassled enables them to make a better decision. If the same customers that had made themselves familiar with what they want to buy have to visit the particular stores over the weekend, it is like being armed with the right information, and their decision will not go wrong for the most part. They do not have to come two or three times, to compare prices and qualities, and they can do it in one stop that is if they have not made the purchase on the Internet using their credit card. Whichever way we look at it, the Internet has become such a unique medium, which has outdone the traditional promotional methods like catalogue advertising, for example. Who will go back to that route when an overwhelming amount of information could be had on the Internet with much relative ease and comfort?

What is key here is the number of people surfing the Internet is very high, it has reached the one billion mark, and a good number of them could be ready to buy if they find what they are exactly looking for. This assumption itself will get blurred because people are found to be impulse-buyers too, which is a bonanza that raises the stake for those who are promoting their products and services on the Internet. Because it is possible to catch the eyeballs of unprecedented number of surfers if one has a presence on the Internet with the right product and service. In addition, those who have a very efficient presence on the Internet will be the most benefited ones. Therefore, why would it be difficult to sell whatever is on hand when one finds oneself in the midst of a huge marketplace that is accessible by global buyers. No more depending on local buyers only. No more serving your small town customers only, even if the number of buyers of a decent small town could be overwhelming, for example, over the weekend or on the holiday season.

Hence, for starters, if anyone has a product or a service to sell that is the place to be, but one has to be equipped with the right procedure of doing business on the Internet. Otherwise, sinking any amount of money to get started, or having that great product or service, or spending 20 hours a day might not generate any sales at all, and those will be the sizzling issues that we will discuss as we go along.

We have heard about the Internet being a great place to be in, but is it really possible to make money? We will address this question eventually. People do not necessarily have to have their own product or service to make money on the Internet, and say, "Gee I have never had anything to sell, so how am I going to make money?" There are many ways to find things to do, or there are products and services that are offered on the Internet to sell, provided that there is that need to make money, and the end result is those who harness what is offered end up making money. But everyone who is parting wisdom about making money on the Internet warns that it is not a get-rich-quick scheme, but few might have gotten lucky by simply getting their fingers on the right combination.

For the most part considering, spotting, or finding the exact things to do, the aspect of getting established, the aspect of promoting a business, and the aspect of being found by the big number of surfers are the key issues that will make a big difference. It could cost an arm and a leg as there are hordes of services, like what we are dong here for example, that promise to help anyone get started. For the most part a considerable amount of success could be attained by following the directions set by these savvy sources, but with the same token there could be a shoddy guidance or a guidance that does not measure up, so it is beware users right from the start.

It is a known fact that an effective promotional method could generate sales by enticing people into action who otherwise would have been passive onlookers, because there are a lot of people with a lot of money and they do not know what is up for grabs that they can use. Fair and square, there are businesses who believe they know what is good and useful for everyone. These two groups will meet nowhere else other than on the Internet. An effective marketer could give a good value for buyers and reap a reward for the service, and if the business is a well-maneuvered undertaking, the reward will add up.

That is when we hear so-and-so have ended up making so much money, but that is the end part of the story. The beginning part of the story is that particular seller might have gone through a strict regiment of disciplines for a long time, maybe for a full year. Because that is how long it could take to start generating income for some, although some might make money quickly, and in most cases being benefited immensely is the direct outcome of a hard work with those few nagging exceptions.

Consequently, if you are planning to start using this relatively new medium to make money, you have come to the right place. It does not matter whether you have a winning product or service, it does not matter whether you are a biz-whiz, it does not matter whether you have experience in marketing or not, it does not matter whether you have a lot of money or not, as long as you want to make money doing something on the Internet the possibilities are unlimited. That is what we will be covering in detail as we go along. If you are ready with the perseverance, you will see good results within three to six month's time. We will explain why it will take that long, but you could start enjoying what you will be doing from day one. Because people enjoy hobbies and they do them day in and day out. If you know someone who had made it faster than that, they could be the exceptions or something extraordinary might have come their way. So, tune in for the remaining section that will give you a run for your money.

It Is not like Brick-and-Mortar

The first thing you will notice is it is not like brick-and-mortar business, because it is or it is not possible to have customers flocking to your site from day one. The same thing is applicable in the brick-and-mortar case. If you are selling a product or you are giving a service, in the case of the brick-and-mortars you will open shop mostly in a designated business district where buyers will come to do shopping. There are many these kinds of districts scattered all over the place if you take the case of a given location. Some are concentrated while some are scattered sparingly, but shoppers know how to find them.

One way buyers can find businesses is if they advertise, by telling people at the spot where the business is taking place or what the business is doing so that it will be easy for the buyers to find the business. A business located in a busy business district has always a better chance of making more money say, for example, than a business that is located in an area where there is no traffic of big buyers. Those businesses that are doing business outside of the business-designated areas are after residents of a given area in almost all cases. Unless there is a good number of people living in a given area it does not make sense to start any business that is selling products or services, because the chance of buyers coming by seeing the ad put outside only is slim. However, the rule of thumb is open your business where buyers and customers could find the business and there is no need to spend money for advertising because the location itself will bring the buyers.

Doing business on the Internet is a little bit different, but, more or less, the basic principle is the same. You have to start out with something that has demand, but when it comes to location, it does not matter. What counts is to be on "cyberspace" and what makes doing business different on the Internet is a business has to advertise a lot in order to be found. When the success rate of a brick-and-mortar business depends on the nature of the business and the location, the business on the Internet depends on advertising, because that is how a business can drive traffic to its site, which is the shop.

There are spots where you can take and park you business doing the same thing like the brick-and-mortars and you can advertise your business so that buyers will come to your site. Some of these kinds of locations are directories and cyber malls. They play the same role location plays in brick-and-mortar business and some of them charge to be included in their list, some are free and all it takes is to get registered. It is known that people who are savvy about the Internet will go directly to directories and cyber malls, click on the category of the goods and services they are looking for, and most of the time there will a good number of businesses that are offering what they are looking for. But it is important to know these directories and cyber malls as their number is on the rise, and all of them do not have relevance. They could play a more important role than search engines, but knowing the good ones is key for both buyers and sellers, and businesses could get the same amount of traffic from directories that they can get from search engines.

But one of the problem is there could be a good number of businesses doing the same thing like in the brick-and-mortar case, and some kind of fluke with good reliable service and quality of products, with a better pricing than the competitor could be the few attractions that might distinguish similar businesses.   As a result, there is nothing difficult about registering one's business in a directory or a cyber mall and see what kind of traffic could be generated from there.

There are things both have to do in their turn, in order to have a good rank in the search engine results, because that is part of doing business. Even if they do not, what is required of a business is to follow their procedure and go through the process of registering the business with the search engines. There are hundreds of them out there and registering in most of them will make the possibility of finding the business easy. There is this myth that says, doing business is easier to those who are already established as brick-and-mortar because they could be a household name, and there is a whole lots of truth in it, because the cyber presence will serve as another outlet to the point where people can find them by their household name. However, it is also possible to do business independent of having a brick-and-mortar household name status and that is where things will become a bit difficult and complicated.

The whole idea is not very much separated from doing business in the real world, except that the cyberspace avails much more opportunity than being limited to serve a given market or locality. The art of availing oneself to the Internet surfers whose number is approaching one billion is getting complicated by the day. Consequently, what will render result is to choose what to do first and then to do it the right way.

Before touching on what to do, we have to ascertain ourselves that it is possible to do business on the Internet and make money, in some case better than the brick-and-mortars, because the key ingredients are; first it is a known fact that the number of people who are willing to buy on the Internet is on the rise. Secondly, the variety of the products and the services people are willing to buy on the Internet is also on the rise. Third the risk of being swindled is going down as the vendors and those who are processing the transaction on their behalf have an agreement between them, where protecting the customer's interest should be given the priority. Whereas, if there is a customer dissatisfaction, making a refund is possible, as well as in case the product is not received the transaction will be reversed in due course that requires following a certain procedure within a given period of time, and there is a dispute solving mechanism in place if both parties are interested.

Because of this arrangement, businesses tend to be more careful even if it is difficult to say that it will be totally immune of swindlers. Some financial services keep record of the disputes that had taken place and warn buyers about the reputation of the business which will go a long way to oblige business owners to do their business at the at most strict integrity level.

Consequently, as long as there is a plain level field for both sellers and buyers, there is no need why they should not interact, because both of them will derive a certain advantage. For the sellers, doing an effective business on the Internet is a breath of fresh air and cost effective, a subject we will touch on soon. The same goes for the buyers too, because they will get some advantages either in terms of their time, or they can make a better comparison in a very short period of time as they can have the means at the tip of their finger, in the comfort of their home or workplace. They do not have to drive a long distance to find a particular business that carries what they need, and even some of the businesses might not be available in a given locality, which might require a long drive, which adds to the expense. Let us not forget the price, which is low because Internet business owners do not have the overhead and they can pass that advantage to the consumers.

Today's business districts are clogged with parking shortages, unless the businesses are located in a mall, which means there is going to be parking problem, and there is going to be more expense involved. We do not have to forget the traffic tickets that are always out there too and what they will do to our pocket, maybe if not to our driving records, because the odd is always out there. Why be on the road when we know it that we are taking risk every time we choose to cruise through the traffic, even if it is deemed to be safe for the most part, but still we are taking risk of not only getting involved in an accident, but even getting killed.

There are more realities that are making doing business on the Internet more inviting, because that is the way to go. People were catalogue-shopping before the advent of the Internet, but now shopping on the Internet is becoming a different experience that is only matched by being there in person, because seeing, touching, and possessing what we will buy immediately is possible, but the risks are still there and the Internet is coming to the rescue, and shopping is not going to be an ordeal. Could you imagine taking a car-full of kids to a shop to buy items like clothing and school supplies when all that can be done on a computer screen while the kids themselves are participating and the whole thing could take a few hours, not a long grueling day. So, the advantage is there, and if people were not getting some advantages they will not be flocking to the millions of web sites that are offering all sorts of products and services under the sun. Those who want to take advantage of this explosion, all they have to do is take their proper place under this new sun, and they will not regret the measures they took.

But it is not like the brick-and-mortar, for example, where the minute a business puts a sign outside and is located in a business district, it does not matter whether the business is tending to the need of a given business or residential area, or it is located in a downtown of a given city, as long as those two things come together the business will start doing business immediately. But the Internet is different in that perspective, because there are businesses that had been there, with products or services for years, and they are not selling much while others are making money, some of them a lot of it. This attests to the fact that the Internet is not for everyone, yet it is for everyone if everyone follows a given procedure.

It is unfortunate that it has to be like this, but when comparing what will be spent in a brick-and-mortar business to what will be spent on an Internet business, the Internet business is cheaper. If there is more laboring involved, doing business on the Internet could get much cheaper, but it will not come free for the most part, because at least there is a need to pay an internet service provider (ISP) to be connected to the Internet. From there on it is up to the business, because there are a horde of businesses that will promise to help a business become successful in what it is doing, and some are darn expensive, that is if whatever they are trying to sell is workable and help a business better sell on the Internet. Some are affordable and as what they are charging is less, the solution they are offering could also be at the lower ebb. Yet, if the business is determined to see good result and have the time, all it might have to do is roll its sleeves and devote a given number of hours a day, a week, a month, and it could see itself laughing to the bank.

Therefore, anyone can start a business and could hand over the promoting part of the job to others and fork out whatever they will charge, start comparing the cost, and see if the business will break even. Or make it half-half, where the business will exert some effort, but still it will have to spend some money to take advantage of what is out there in terms of making a business viable and profitable. On the other hand, the business will do things for the most part and it might have to spend some money for the minimum necessities, but it should not allow anyone to cost it an arm and a leg.

The job of this book is to help the startups evaluate which might be good for a particular case, because it is possible to make the business' presence felt by the buyers immediately that is, as fast as the brick-and-mortars and see a horde of traffic come to the business' site. However, to do so there are expensive ways and there are affordable ways. If the startup is novice to the Internet business, it will be difficult to distinguish which is which, and because of the naivete, others could feast upon the startup. One way of avoiding that is to do the required homework, more than anything else. Because, the business world as we know it could be dog-eat-dog unless care is taken at every step of the process. A business can afford to pay for whatever is on offer and once the payment is complete, a handshake takes place. Whatever was it paid for will have better utilization if the payer is more informed, and in most cases if the payer were more informed it might have not incurred some of the expenses. Therefore, it is good to separate the chaff from the wheat, and it is undeniable that there are numerous guides offering material littering the Internet. Some are very expensive, although what they are offering is not different from those that are affordable. However, they might have equivalent or in some cases better solutions.

It is unfortunate that, because cyberspace is the by-product of technology, it is not a complete product at all, it is still evolving, but there are parts that are working rendering certain outcome, and that is what people are taking advantage of. The innovations directed at the technology are emerging from various directions, which means there is not a single entity that is responsible for cyberspace. What drives everything as usual is the profit motive and everyone is wracking their brain to come up with workable products on a daily basis. These new findings, some of them make a big difference, and give for those who utilize them the proper way a lot of advantages, whereas those who are not utilizing them properly will lose out.

As a result, it does not make sense to only want to do business on the Internet, but knowing how to do it effectively is the key. That depends heavily on how one is familiar with the latest developments. That by itself has become a full time occupation for some and they are making a full time living out of it, because specialization still works. A newbie who wants to start business on the Internet is always advised to try the water gradually, because it does not make sense to quit one's job to devote full time for the Internet venture without being sure that it is possible to generate income on the Internet.

Most probably, that is what the marvel of the Internet is. Anyone with a computer and Internet connection can try the water, and for sure, some percentage of all those amateur adventures might someday generate their livelihood solely on the Internet alone. But until achieving that peak point, they have to seek an expert's advice, which is scattered all over the place on the Internet. If they know how to find it or save time by spending money that they will spend on a lunch, to look out for a guidance that could end up letting them into the know-how to carve their future fortune, it will be their worthwhile.

As a conclusion of this chapter, we can summarize that there is a stark similarity between doing business in the real world and on cyberspace, because the basic chemistry is more or less the same. What is different is the execution process and each one of them has its own advantages. At this point it is difficult to say which one is having the upper hand, as mostly cyberspace is considered to be another outlet to those who are doing brick-and-mortar business, yet there are some who have defied the fact that a good profitable business could be done on the Internet as a stand-alone business. But because it is not easy and can be disappointing, even expensive and draining, it requires a good amount of preparation before contemplating to open shop on cyberspace. It is possible to make the right mental preparation through this book and make yourself familiar with the numerous pitfalls to save yourself from aggravation.

The Hands-On Phase

Now we are approaching the no-nonsense zone and we should have asked ourselves what we want to do on the Internet. The good thing about it is, we can come up with our own idea or we can scour the net to find what to do, because there are many that are offering things to do, and they pay for whatever service is rendered for them. So first, let us start with those who could come up with their own idea. Almost anything can be done on the Internet, from selling perishable goods like produce, foods, flowers to durable goods of all kind and size, like jumbo jets or nuts and bolts, because they could be delivered anywhere in the world, even if there is a price tag attached to it. Moreover, it is the price that will make people think twice. Unless the product is unique, why not go to a local shop and do the buying in person. Yet, because of the lower overhead involved while doing business on the Internet, goods and services should be cheaper than at the brick-and-mortars.

Why not we take Amazon for example, because it is the best example, and it has proven that there is market for almost anything. Why would people choose to buy books that require shipping to a given address over the Internet instead of picking them from local bookstores? The answers could be numerous, but how about if someone lives in a remote area where a good bookstore is not available, which is very true in North America, and these kinds of individuals could find themselves where they are living for various reasons. It is possible that they could be locals there or they are there in business or are there because of relocation, but if they want to buy good quality books they will have to go to the bigger towns or cities. How many of the bigger towns have bookstores that carry the recent books? Not many of them unfortunately. If the towns do not have them people will have to wait until they drive to the cities that could be once a year, and in between, they could miss out a lot. The same is applicable for many products that are not available in many out of the way areas.

So what is the solution? The Internet has become the best solution, because as long as there is a phone line it is possible to access the Internet for a miniscule amount of money, then all it takes is to log into Amazon or any other company and browse for as many books or goods as one wants to buy. And let us not forget Amazon alone is carrying much more products, pay with a credit card, and within two weeks or so time, dozens of quality books or other sizzling products that would have taken a year and maybe driving hundreds of miles are at the doorstep, either by a courier service or through the postal service.

Amazingly enough, Amazon is competing with brick-and-mortars in the bigger cities, and in order to attract business they have to compete. One way to beat those stores is to charge a lower price, because they can afford it, since they do not have the same overhead. They do not have to rent a storefront; they do not have to staff the stores with dozens of employees because of the automated work. All this gives them room to charge lesser amount, which is good for the consumers, because they will never spend more than they will be spending in a storefront shop.

Therefore, what this shows is this analysis is applicable to almost any commodity we can think of. It is not only that, in the real world it takes a while to find the best shops, because people flock to the known ones. However, there are small establishments that are opening by the dozen and even if they can do business because of the location only, unless they advertise heavily they could remain small and unknown. What determines their ability to advertise is their capital and their volume of business. If they have a big volume of business and they see a lot of goods out their door, they would counteract that by bringing in more goods through their door, and eventually it is a business that has a large volume of sales that becomes successful and profitable. If this chemistry does not visit a business it will disappear at the same speed it surfaced. The main reason could be bad location and low volume of business, assuming that the other required factors of doing business are in place.

However, on cyberspace it is different, for one, the expense is much lower, even taking advertising into consideration. Because all known overhead expenses will disappear and what attracts customers is advertising, which is affordable for the most part, and somehow it is made affordable. To an extent, having one's web site optimized properly could even bring down the advertising expense. For a site that sells hot products the recommendation is to mix different kinds of advertising methods, as there are a huge number of search engines, web sites, and reciprocal links that will drive traffic to a particular site. However, the majority of searches are done on the major search engines, such as Google, Yahoo, MSN, Ask, and AOL, where two of them have a very effective and, more or less, affordable advertising method that is recommended and MSN is also catching up. There are smaller search engines that have similar or a little bit different advertising in place that we will discuss thoroughly as we continue with our effort to do an effective business on the Internet.

Consequently, it is not out of whack at all if we presume that, anyone who wants to go into business should look at the Internet first. Because it is eliminating all the traditional barriers as it avails the business for up to close to billions of buyers, not only locally or continent wise, but globally, a phenomenon that had not been thought of. It was only catalogue selling that was reaching that big a customer base, but still there is a problem and an expense involved while distributing the catalogue. Some localities might not get it if they are located outside of the North America region, even in NA in some cases. It could also have been difficult to do business in another country as close neighbor as Canada for example, but now the Chinese can use their credit card or any other paying method and expect to receive their goods at their address within two to three weeks time. Even if cyberspace is the extension of catalogue selling, it adds much more capabilities and covers territories that were unthinkable before.

When it comes to making payments there was no way one can use a credit card to pay for a purchase in real time because of the distance involved. It is possible to do it over the phone, yes, but that will add more expense for both the seller and buyer unless the seller provides 1 800 number, and it is the buyer who will pay for it because it will be added on the price of the goods. But on the Internet, that is one of the many expenses that will not accrue or becomes nominal making the products cheaper.

Simply following a proven method of doing business on the Internet could have all these and that method is evolving by the day. We do not know what new things are evolving as we write here, for example, or what the new introductions will be in due course, and all it takes is tuning in into what is taking place. It is possible to say that once the business is set up properly it is as good as leaving it on auto pilot and the cyber shop will sell the products while the owner is sleeping, or doing other things, vacationing, on a 7/24/ basis. All that is required from the part of the business owner is to do a regular follow up.

But when it gets busy it might require more time and because the business is making more money it can afford to hire help, or it will tough it up by its own until it cannot do so. At one point it will hire help or truncate some part of the business because it cannot handle it because of lack of staff. This is not an overblown hot balloon, because all sorts of products are being bought and sold on the Internet. We are talking tangible products here hand-in-hand with services, of course, and when we talk about downloadable products the possibilities are even much higher and it is a totally new phenomenon. In the tangible world a business can sell anything, locally, or continental wise, or globally. Electronic products of any size, clothing that are difficult to find where they are hidden if buyers hit the pavement searching for them in the brick-and-mortar shops, household products, size unrestricted like washers, refrigerators, stoves, cars, jumbo jets, and the list is unlimited.

If you can buy them you can sell them too and all your business has to do is make itself available for business by following fine-tuned and tried procedures. Once a business starts selling on the Internet, it would not want to try to sell in a storefront because it will immediately feel that there is a confinement to a minute segment of the market.

So where is the best place to start? While deciding what to sell, is it going to be one item, or are there going to be a number of items? Who will be the supplier? This is a key since the business has to have adequate supply, but it can start with a small quantity. The owner can use a garage, a living room, or an extra bedroom for storage, because it does not make sense to go out and rent storage before the startup is certain that the business has taken off.

After that, the job will be done through an effective web site for the most part that we will talk about, or the startup can rent a mall front as we mentioned it earlier. No kidding, it is possible to have a mall front, and the advantage is it is the mall owner that does the advertising for the startup, and it is like the real world mall where people know its existence. If it had been made popular, people are flocking to it because they know they will find what they are looking for, and there are more outlets like directories that will work hand-in-hand with an effective web site. There are also independent sellers where advertising a business is possible. There are sites that are very popular like Click Bank for example where putting a downloadable product is possible. Because people know it and it is just a matter of visiting the site to browse what is available. Other less popular sites might have to advertise a lot and having a link on their site if not a product will drive traffic to a selling site, and that is why they charge a fee to advertise a product or some of them could be free, but a link is different.

However, we will talk about links when we start talking about how to drive traffic to a site the key source of business, which will enable the startup to take full control of the business instead of depending on someone else. Even if there is nothing wrong with it, how about if they are not doing what is necessary, yet they are charging money? They say they are advertising, the business takes their word, but there is no result, and the money spent on this kind of business could stay in the startup's own pocket or it is possible to spend it on an advertising campaign. That is why it is recommended to do a through research about any business a startup is doing business with. Yet, even better, with a few methods of advertising that will give a leg-up to any business, webmasters and marketers could take charge of their web site to sell independently or hand-in-hand with others, as it could be a better means of generating sales.

To summarize what we touched on, it is up to the webmaster to come up with what to do and how to do it, at least at this point, even if we will make suggestions and comparisons as we go along. Another essential point here is after surpassing a certain point, the supply aspect of the business will have to be in place. This means a given amount of inventory should always be at hand instead of running to obtain the goods. It is important to do the delivery at the promised timeframe, no matter what kind of delivery system is the option

There is also how to process the payments as there are a number of them, and we will discuss them when the time is right. Then we have to depend heavily on the unavoidable advertising, which requires spending money, which is the responsibility of the business. The more time spent on the business, the success rate will be much higher, and as well as curtailing the expense is possible. When this becomes reality, the amount of profit that will be realized will be much higher, the main motivation for going through all the trouble. Keep tuning in as we have passed the warm-up threshold and things will start to get a bit complicated, but first we will deal with those who are planning to sell digital products on the Internet, which is becoming phenomenal, because depending on the product if the market is out there, the amount of profit to generate could be astonishing.

Digital Products

When it comes to digital products, it is possible to say that the Internet and the computers themselves are in existence to accommodate this particular venue more than anything else is. At the same time, even if some portion of the work is similar, especially the advertising part of the job, the delivery part is almost expense free, because it is possible to do it electronically, in real time. There is no waiting time involved because downloading it off the Internet is possible at the time of making the payment. And the payment system is made easy for all kinds of payments, where all one needs is a credit card, a debit card, an electronic check, a withdrawal from one's account, and, of course, buyers can remit the money to the seller through the mail or bank wire, which are a bit expensive and require some time. No matter, taking care of business is possible and had never been easy.

All sort of companies are offering a payment method. Companies like PayPal, for example, make doing business a breath of fresh air, because they are affordable and have a state of the art technology that does not require any payment except a low commission whenever money is sent or received. There are dozens of this kind of companies that one can look for on the Internet.

Or it is possible to access the service of a merchant account provider, which offers more or less the same service, with a much higher fees that has made them less popular, but are as reliable as the other ones and a must for more complicated transactions where kind and high volume turnover is involved.

What digital products are available to download in real time? There are all sorts of software that have a resale price attached to them after making the initial payment. This kind of business depends on how hot the item is and on the amount of advertisement involved. Because all it takes is to bring qualified visitors to the site and make them buy the product. We will talk about how to bring these qualified visitors economically to a site that is doing business, although the shortcut is advertising.

Of course, when you advertise, even if it is effective there is the possibility of missing out from some sources that could be obtained by marketing what one is doing. However, the difference is if one wants to advertise say, for example, with Google and Yahoo, the assumption is, between them, the two sites alone attract up to 80 percent of those who search the internet, which will make it a safe bet where if someone engages in advertising with them the chances of being found is certain and high. But, for some, the expense might be unbearable, because there is a lot of competition in a form of bidding that could drain resources. One solution is to mix paid advertising with the other marketing systems we will discuss as we go along. If those marketing efforts can bring a site into the first 20 and 30 results, the chance of doing business will get better. The problem is there are millions of sites that are competing for these particular hot spots where those who are conducting search will go to. Even if up to the first 100 search results might have a chance to do business and their chance of getting a good rank will get better as the spot where they pop up gets higher.

Consequently, doing business on the Internet is not simply opening shop; it has more to do with marketing. At times, advertising itself might not cut it for most, but because a well-done marketing has a staying power, it would make a difference in the long-run.

The other key issue is some products sell themselves because they have demand, but they need effective marketing as there are many vendors soliciting sales for them. The crucial game here is how to get one's fair share. It is possible, for example, to sell ebooks that have demand on the Internet and a good number of them have a resale right. However, how they are packaged and presented makes a big difference.

There are businesses that will hand down a well made turnkey where all sellers have to do is pay the fee, assume a right of the well-built web site, go out and make their own marketing that is in addition to the network exposure some of them avail. Products themselves do not sell, but if there is an exception, it is that in the long-run, the search engines will find the site without any effort made by the owner of the site. They will index it, and if it is a well-built site and meets the requirements, it could be a candidate to get a good rank. Because that is all it takes to get a good rank on search engines. But the fact of the matter is it takes a long time to make it there if the right amount of effort is not exerted. Even then, some tweaking here and there is required to keep the site updated regularly; otherwise, some search engines will drop it out their directory. It is not a surprise if there are sites that do not get any decent position in the search results, and such a fate is solely dependent on the amount of work that is put into the site.

The same goes while selling one's own writing in a form of ebooks, tutorials, or software, for example. If the right amount of marketing is in place, it is possible to stir interest about a given product. There are myriad of things to do before even starting selling anything online and this could be applicable to any product.

As a conclusion, it is believed that from what had been mentioned above, readers and would be webmasters could realize that it is indeed possible to do business on the Internet and what counts is what kind of effort is exerted to promote the business that will avail the end result. It is different from a brick-and-mortar undertaking, because it is not expensive to get started for starters that is if someone is already surfing the Internet looking for information or to pursue a hobby, because they do not have to buy at least the most expensive equipment, which is a computer. And today, as we know it, a new desktop costs only around $500 or $600, and buying a state of the art new laptop with less than $1000 is possible making even the startup capital miniscule when compared with mortar-and-bricks. The rest is easy as most of it is available free. ISP could cost only $10 and how cheap does it have to get than this?

But if one rents a storefront in a good hot location, it will, of course, cost much more than this, but chances are doing business immediately is also possible, because the customer base knows where to find businesses due to the location. Customers might be on the lookout for other vendors to compare price and quality. If the individual does not want to do the job or they cannot do it alone because of the volume of the business, they will have to hire someone. However, automation might make hiring more staff unnecessary in most cases while doing business online.

Brick-and-mortars, whether they can afford it or not, when the business volume picks up they have to hire more staff. Let us not forget stocking the store well, for instance, because businesses cannot keep ten items of every product and plan to restock as they run low. The possibility that they can run low is imminent if the store is located on a good area. In addition, it does not look good for the incoming customers, when the store is deserted, because it is not customary, and people could think a lot of things, like what could be lacking in this thinly spread-out products? Are they parody goods? Or is there some kind of illegal activity involved? The outcome could be, instead of being worried to death for not doing the wrong thing, the customers will decide to go to the other stores that seem to be meeting the requirements, expectations, and the norms. Because of relevant problems of this kind, starting a storefront requires having a substantial capital.

On the Internet, the business does not even have to have the products nearby, and it all depends on the arrangements put in place because there are different possibilities. The simple one will be the window of two weeks delivery time will give enough time to send the order to the supplier in real time and let the supplier worry about the supplying aspect of the goods. The business sends the payment minus the service charge or commission to the supplier. At times, doing everything automatically is possible, and when the business closes the deal, the supplier will find out. If the business has to receive payment in advance there might be a procedure to follow, but if it is done periodically, the product will go out, and according to the arrangement the middleman will get the commission.

Why would an online business win? It is due to marketing a site effectively. That is what affiliate programs are, where the affiliate works hard to make the site visible and let the rest be taken care of by the amount of ad that is on the site including the copy and the seller's banner. If many people look at it, it is a given that some of them will click through it, and some among those who click through it will buy the product. The affiliate will get the commission and this is one kind of an arrangement where it is the seller that collects the payment, because the sales take place on the seller's web site. That seller could work for a bigger supplier that can keep track of those who sell its products on its behalf.

The other thing is even if it might eat into the spare time of the webmaster that could have been spent with the family or relaxing or doing what one enjoys doing most, in the long run it is possible to keep the up-keeping cost low once the site is set up properly and is launched. It does not need the webmaster or someone else on a regular basis to tend for it. Once a transaction has taken place buyers understand that they will have to wait at least for two-weeks to get what they paid for and will not be worried if they get a confirmation email within 24 hours, and even that could be eliminated by using auto responders. It is not only that those companies like PayPal that are handling the payment almost always send out confirmation email when someone makes a payment.

It even gets better when what is involved is a digital product, as doing the business automatically with no one's involvement is possible. The buyer pays the money through whatever method is setup on the site; the money processor will receive the money, and will direct it into the business' account. It will then send out an email and a detailed description of what took place for both the buyer and the seller. The buyer had downloaded the product that he or she paid for and maybe if he or she is courteous he or she could send out a thank you email for the seller. Doing thousands of this kind of business without being involved at all is possible. What the business does is see the total amount of sales generated for the day or at various intervals. All this is possible because of a proper marketing campaign and as we go along we will be more detailed about some of the actions that a web site has to take, while at the same time examining what kind of marketing schemes are out there in detail. Without them, closing a deal will not at all materialize.

Web Site

We have been beating around the bush for quite a while now and let us get to it, because there is no avoiding it. If you want to start doing business on the Internet, you need an Internet Service Provider (ISP) and you can find them for as low as $10, as long as you have a regular phone connection. However, in order to use the Internet effectively a faster telephone connection known as DSN or broadband is the better choice and it costs a little bit higher. The reason is it takes a long time for the various material to download to the computer of the surfers. There is no better explanation to give except that the speed the digitized documents travel through the phone lines is slow, mainly due to congestion, but the DNS or broadband connection makes that much faster. Yet using cable is highly recommended in areas where there is cable service because it is much faster for the same reason, there is no congestion, the cable line is much wider, and it can also handle much more traffic. But if there is a catch it could also be clogged if there is too much traffic using it, but because of less usage chances are most cable systems are free of congestion for now, but we do not know about the future.

Once the connection is there whatever arrangement is used, what comes next is a web site that is unless a webmaster is selling from someone else's storefront known as malls. They can provide a storefront on their own platform and it is possible to start selling from there directly, but still there has to be an Internet connection, and when that is the case having one's own web site might not be needed. Otherwise, webmasters need their own site, and the first key requirement is it has to be professional looking. That is without talking about the functionality of the web site itself to sell products and services from. The reason why it should look professional is first impression works everywhere and it tells buyers whether the seller is real or shoddy. It has some truth in it although it is not always true, because some startups, simply to save money when they get started, might choose to work from a plain web site that could be made up from a simple text word document converted into an html document and uploaded to the Internet.

They can argue that, as long what is on sale is clearly visible, why does a web site have to have bells and whistles? This issue had been proven when research was made and the truth of the matter is if a business wants to do business it has to do it as a pro. The cost is not that high or it can even be done free as there a good number of sites providing free templates, but still the free services do not come close to those done professionally. The reason might be it is difficult to come up with a professional looking web site and that is why it costs money. There used to be times where sophisticated web sites for big corporations used to cost into the million dollars, but that time had passed quickly, and now for around $100 a decent looking, yet creatively done site could be put at one's disposal.

Even better, there are sites such as Yahoo, Angelfire, and many others that offer their own templates with a free web hosting service, and a better site than that can be drawn on a plain document can be constructed. Yahoo for example has a wizard like most of them to even build a more sophisticated web site free of charge, but it is not only clumsy, the end result somehow dose not measure up with those made professionally. Yet there are some good ones and searching for them could avail a lot of choice. Here, one thing to understand is web development by itself is one huge industry that hires a big number of talented people and they have created a standard that everyone has to use in order to be taken seriously and digressing from that could backfire on the business.

Therefore, the best way to go is to designate a web design expense as a start up cost and once the site's design has taken place there is no looking back. It could also come with a logo or mostly logos also have their own cost because there are others who can design logos and they charge money too. But since these are a few onetime expenses that could last for several years that is until a better web site is required for whatever reason, there will not be any harm done since they could last for a long time. Nevertheless, those who know html can save themselves a lot of trouble, because for the most part that is what it takes to design a professional looking web site.

Once the web site is ready most ISPs provide a space where it could be uploaded or there are a good number of services that includes the major search engines that provide free space to upload a web site and what it requires is to register with them. They also provide a free email service that could go hand-in-hand with the web site. If there is a catch with these kinds of web sites that provide free space, they have to advertise on the web site to offset the cost they incur for providing the free space. That for sure will clutter the page sometimes making it slow to download. Most of them also have popup ads, because this relationship is mutual where those who are providing the free space want sites to display their ads on their site, whereas those who want a free space to upload their site to will get their free space.

However, if what is involved is a good business it is much better to pay for web hosting services which could cost as low as $3 a month depending on the amount of bandwidth the site will require. In addition, with web hosting a site needs a domain name that sometimes comes with the web hosting service free. If the webmaster wants to buy a domain name it is possible to pay a little bit more than $3 and it will be good for the whole year. At the end of the year, it requires renewing and it is possible to do the renewing through whoever arranged the buying of the domain name. However, if a webmaster gets a free space to upload a site at the many services that provide free space for simply registering, the domain name the webmaster chooses will be a sub domain name of the free web hosting service, which is unfit for professionals, but good for personal web sites.

For example, if a webmaster uses Angelfire, the domain name will be www.angelfire.com/nameofthesite.html. The same goes with Yahoo where the domain will be www.geocities.com/nameofthesite.html, which means it does not look professional and most people will know where the hosting is taking place. Not only that they also know it is free, which means it is a sign of not doing well. This definitely could drive business away, because if the webmasters claim to be in business, charging what they are charging if they cannot afford their own web hosting and domain name that will cost as little as what was mentioned above for a month, whatever they are doing might not measure up. Because using anything free means not doing well, so unless it is a hobby those kinds of sites are not good for business. But when the webmaster pays the money for the service that will facilitate the registering of a domain name the site will have com, biz, net, org, or more of the other available suffixes and the domain name will look like www.thesite.com or www.thesite.biz, and so on.

However, one point worth mentioning is there are sites that allow using a domain name, for example. What that means is if the webmaster wants to buy a domain name, which could sometimes be arranged by the same site that provide the free service, or using the other sites that arrange the buying and selling of a domain name, there is a system in place to use a professional looking domain name while using the free service. That is a good disguise but it will not save the site from being bombarded with ads, because that is how the free web hosting providers are making up for what they are providing free.

Another thing to know about domain names is they are like commodities, they can be bought and sold on the market and on auctions, because anyone can go and buy domain names by paying the going price that will not be more than $9 in most cases. There are sites where you can enter the domain name you want to buy and you can find out if the name is available or not and if you like it you can buy that name on the spot. They can also be parked somewhere and generate money for the owner, as there are sites that do that and one of them is www.godaddy.com

Now, the catch is there are people that had been buying key domain names say for example like www.homebusiness.com and they will put it on sale. If someone wants to promote a home business someday on the Internet and wants to use "homebusiness" as a domain name, they can buy it from these kinds of individuals who buy and sell domain names. Otherwise they can settle for other less exacting names like www.home-business.com or any other, and chances are even "home-business" might have been bought and their chance of talking about "homebusiness" could be by using something like www.home-business22.com, which will do the job, but still it is not that perfect name for exactly what they will be doing. The price charged for such domain names could be exorbitant sometimes, which will make buying anything that comes close to what will be done is the way out in order to avoid forking out thousands of dollar, even the not-so-hot names could go for several hundred dollars. And mind you, they paid for them in most cases less than $10, and there are businesses paying a big amount of money just to get that perfect domain name for their business.

One other reason why the domain name is important is it helps with the search result, which shows keywords could be secondary. If the domain name for a bookseller is www.bookseller.com, whenever some one searches for book seller, the chance that this site will pop up is very much high. It even gets better for those who can use one word for their domain name even if generalizing it is unavoidable, and it is like saying www.book.com, for example. The site will pop up with any search made using the word book, but it could be doing so many book related things and the ones that are specific with what they are doing can come up ahead of it. However, for some reason, search results favor one-word keywords even if the others also will not fall short.

When it comes to the amount of bandwidth used, if the site starts attracting too much traffic it should upgrade for a package that can handle more bandwidth. Most hosting companies have different packages based on the amount of bandwidth and the amount of space they provide. Otherwise, when surpassing the bandwidth paid for the site will not be available, they will take it down. Amazingly enough, among those that are providing the free service there are some that offer unlimited bandwidth, but do not count on it, they are overselling. If the site gets a big number of visitors, because it is going to eat into their own bandwidth they will put a cap on it. But it is easy to find out what kind of bandwidth is required and make the arrangement accordingly.

Even if a professionally made web site is recommended it will have to be easy to navigate without being cluttered, because if surfers do not find what they are looking for with a minimal effort, the possibility is they will leave the site without doing anything. This means, professional looking does not necessarily mean a very difficult site to navigate through. Here, it is important to keep search engines in mind too when the site is being constructed, because it will have to be robot-friendly, and web designs with frames will have to be avoided in most cases because some robots can not navigate through them, which means such web sites might not be indexed. Also keeping in mind that the robots only read texts is important, because if there were too many graphics on a web page, their job definitely would be difficult.

Once the web site is ready and uploaded and is made available on the Internet, the next thing to do is to submit it to the various search engines. There are services that will do the submitting free, whereas there are some that will charge money. Also the major search engines allow anyone to submit their site and they have a link on their web sites that says "submit your site". That is, in fact, the shortest and surest way of submitting your site for the major search engines. But as you will find out there are a big number of smaller search engines, directories, and indexes that many surfers do not interact with or come across because they are not popular, or could be specialized to a particular sector, but they still have visitors and submitting to them also is recommended. There are services that will charge a few dollars and would promise to submit the site to thousands of search engines, directories, and indexes, and at times it is worth trying them.

The problem with site submitting is the bigger search engines will send out their robots frequently to scour for new material on the Internet and they visit already indexed sites that change their contents regularly. This means if a site does not change its content frequently they will label it as inactive or dormant site and will be placed in a secondary index known as "dead zone". Even if they do not cancel it, it might not show in the search results at a favorable position, and we will touch on this subject as we go along. Here we are just showing the difference between the bigger search engines, which would label a site inactive or dormant, whereas the smaller ones if a site is not submitted regularly, in fact, on a monthly basis they will cancel it, and this is the major difference.

In addition, submitting a site more than once a month is spamming and it will instigate a penalty by the bigger search engines and of course, the smaller search engines will cancel or ban a site, but they are more tolerant where some of them encourage it because it will save them from canceling sites. Consequently, doing submission once a month is enough and essential. There are services that will do the follow up for a fee and is worth looking them up, as there are a good number of them. At the same time, as long as the web site is on the Internet and it does not restrict access to visiting robots, the search engines will eventually index it without submitting it for anyone of them. But it is only the bigger search engines that crawl the Internet by their own, as the small ones will have to be made to send out their robots, because they might not crawl the overall Internet.

The bigger search engines such as Google, Yahoo, and MSN have their own special requirements that are worth knowing. Google for example has what it calls algorithm, and it is a criterion to meet in order to index a site and make it available in the search results at a favorable position. Among the things the major search engines are looking for are reciprocals links. Reciprocal links are when sites that are doing, more or less, similar things agree to swap links, which means if the other site is willing to display the link of the other site, the other one will also be willing to do the same by putting the link on their site. When the robots visit both sites at different occasions they will find out that they are pointing at each other, and if there is relevance with what they are doing, even a general resemblance is accepted, it will be a plus for being indexed quickly and getting a good rank. The link exchange will have to be with a big number of similar web sites. The recommended minimum is 50 reciprocal links.

There is no ceiling except that new web sites have to do it gradually. The reason why search engines made such a requirement is it is possible to do it overnight by hiring certain services that are specializing in creating reciprocal links to sites. Literally, for a fee, they could create hundreds or thousands of reciprocal links overnight, and most of the time the relevancy issue could also be there.

There are also a good number of software products that could do it by automating the submitting process and one good software to do that it seoelite.com. The way to do it is by finding out who the competing web sites are by simply doing a search for the keywords a site is using. Those that are at the top of the search results are good targets, because what it takes to do better than them in the search results is to take their place. There is software that can easily find out which sites these web sites are linking with. What comes next is to send to those sites an email asking them if they are willing to exchange links, and thousands of email could be sent at a click of a button. Yet, this recommended process at least takes time and since the software will do all the difficult part of the job, it is just a matter of clicking a button.

That is why search engines came up with this rule where if a site has built reciprocal list quickly it would definitely be bought. It is a known knowledge that there are also sites that are selling links and they are the most quickest fix that will become pointing links the minute money exchanges hands, because these are readymade links waiting to be directed to anyone paying for them.

Even if there is no harm done, since reciprocal links used to be one of the key measuring rods, new sites were buying their way into the top search results, and that was what the major search engines wanted to avoid. There are also sites that get high points especially from Google that has a grading method of web sites based on their popularity, which is measured by the number of sites that are pointing at them or linking with them. Any site that gets linked with these kinds of web sites that have higher popularity points will add to the ranks, where having link with the top popular ones with high points of ten could mean to get indexed very quickly, from several hours to 24 hours.

There are these kinds of sites that have attained the high status and they sell their link. The end result is who would not want to spend say $150 or more and get indexed quickly instead of wait months, because that is how much they charge for a month to be linked with them. After being indexed that being the most important thing if the fee gets expensive, it can be discontinued. However, having a link with such sites that have high popularity points helps even in finding the site at the top of search results. However, since it is expensive, most webmasters prefer to do it by their own, but the fact that there are big businesses that will fork out this kind of money cannot be ruled out, because such sites are catering for such businesses. In the long run, when they attain the rank themselves they can shun away from them.

One other reason behind using the links as a yardstick is the search engines believe that a site well connected with other similar sites manifests that it has authority in what it is doing. However, people's starting buying links defied that and it was possible to build thousands of them overnight. Lately the importance of reciprocal links is waning because once webmasters know what is required they could quietly build the reciprocal links over time, even if they might not have authority in what they are doing.

Another important measuring rod search engines are using is they are looking for relevant content that will be updated regularly that is daily if possible, as all the daily news portals are always on top of search results. Also changing content on a weekly or monthly basis also has its merits, because it will save the site from being labeled as dormant or inactive, and robots will avoid such sites, resulting in their not being shown in search results and would be placed in a second index searchers will not have access to.

Hence, either webmasters can write their own content in a form of articles that has relevance to what the web site is doing or they can have it done by someone else. Or there are a big number of sites that are offering quality free content to use on a web site, but if there is a catch if the content is shown on many other web sites, as mostly the case is with such free available content in the open, there is always a chance of being caught by the robots that can detect duplicate material. When that happens they can penalize a site severely affecting the chance of its being found with search results.

It is also important how the site is constructed and this is the topic of search engine optimization (SEO). What it does is it prepares the site to make it robot friendly and there are experts known as SEOs that will charge a fee to do the job. They will work on a site on a regular basis, because in reality since the algorithms change frequently the sites will have to update themselves in order not to lose out. It requires to hire an SEO company full time if what the site is doing is important, and especially when the rank it gets is important for what it is doing. Or there are simple SEO tactics webmasters themselves can do to make the site robot friendly.

One of the key things professional SEOs know is what kind of keywords are effective for a given web site that is in a given line of trade and that itself can break or make a web site. Yet, webmasters can also do the same thing and if they choose effective keywords they could get top spots on search results, otherwise they will be left out of the key spots. Most search engines have a system that help users choose the best keywords and how it works is by simply typing what a site is doing and the best keywords for what the site is doing could be generated. In other words, those keywords might be what others doing similar things had been using. It also has a second spin where testing each keyword for how frequently it is being used is possible. Here it is possible to observe two things, and one of them is how many times users had been using the particular keyword or if that keyword is overused by other webmasters. For newcomers, what the recommendation is to use phrases instead of one keyword, and we will explain the reason when we start talking about advertising.

Another key aspect of SEO is something known as a "tag" that all search engines are looking for when they visit a site. This tag is where webmasters or SEOs are putting important information about what the site is doing and that is what the search engines display in the search result and if it is missing they could pick anything legible for them on the web site and that is what will be displayed. In most cases when the web designers design the web site, they know some information about what the web site will be doing, and they will insert as part of their web design what the site is doing. The robots will scan it and display it, which could be gibberish most of the time if it is not done correctly. Or those who use wizards to build their web sites, through the questioners asked the users will put what their site is doing and that will be displayed inside a tag.

The way out of this problem is to go to a web site like scrubtheweb.com and use their tag generator.

```
<title>bookseller</title>
<meta http-equiv="Content-Type" content="text/html; charset=us-ascii">
<meta name="Description" content="This site sells the best books available on SEO.">
<meta name="Keywords" content="books, books for sell, books on sell,">
<!-- META Tags Created With: STW META Tag Builder http://www.scrubtheweb.com/abs/ -->
```

And this is what comes out when you use the scrubtheweb.com meta tag generator and you can see it starts with the title, then there is the content where it says what the site is doing, and there are keywords. That is all required except that the title should have the main thing the site is doing because it just happens that it is what the search engines are looking at first. Then the same thing needs repeating in the content by being explicit about what the site is doing so that the search terms will match the content.

The key words also are important although search engines do not come that far, because if they do not find what they are looking for in the title mostly, the site could be dropped, or will be displayed for whatever content the search were able to find. This is a very key issue for webmasters to know. But putting some keywords is practical, in case the search engines want to go that far, which is most unlikely from what is taking place. Nevertheless, making sure keywords will not be stuffed is important, which means they should not be repeated more than three times. For example if "books" is used more than three times it will be considered spamming, the same goes with "sell". Therefore, that aspect requires care.

There are other sites that could be found if search is made using "tag generators", although they do not do anything different. But scrubtheweb.com is simple and what it takes is to paste the html code that is generated on top of the web page, and it does not show on the main web page, but when robots visit the site the first thing they will encounter is what is in the "tag". That is what they scan and put on the search results, because the tag tells the robots what the site is exactly doing. That is the title of the site, a few line of explanation of the site or what is doing, and most importantly keywords that it is using that are relevant to what it is doing, because it is through those keywords the site will be found "theoretically". Nevertheless, sprinkling the main keywords the site is using carefully in the title and in the content would suffice.

Because, for some reason, when search is made the keywords searchers supply the search engines with are compared first with what is included in the title tag and then with the content tag. It is after that the keywords are considered. The truth of the matter is it had been proven that if there are enough keywords in the title and the content tag, those few lines of explanation about what the site is doing, the robots do not bother about the keywords supplied, although they do not say so.

But the possibility is if the search engines did not find enough keywords either in the title tag or in the content they might make a quick search and comparison with the chosen keywords, yet it does not work like that. Because they can use whatever is in the title and content, which means finding the site for what it is doing will go out the window unless care is taken on the outset. However, the safe way out is to put hot keywords in the title tag and in the text as well.

Then there are dos and do nots that webmasters should be aware of when they are optimizing their site. One of them is "cloaking" and even if it is a bit advanced what is involved is those who have the know-how will try to outdo search engines. When the robots visit, what they will encounter is a different page than surfers will encounter. This might be common among sites that worry they might not get a favorable consideration from the robots because of what they might be doing. As a result, especially those who are using SEO service are advised to look out for such arrangements, because some SEOs will use such tactic so that the site will get a good rank, without worrying about its being penalized as they are only paid for enabling a site attain a good rank.

Mini site networks are different pages with a link with the main page, but their optimization is as good as the main web page with their own keywords and tags. The problem with them is a false link-density could be created that could deceive the robots, and this will specially happen when the pages have their own unique URL, not when they are not treated as subordinate pages that will be accessed through the main page. Search engines penalize such techniques and it is only SEOs that can do that to a site without the knowledge of the webmaster.

Link farms have to be avoided as much as possible, especially if they are in a black list by the search engines, even if it is difficult to know for all search engines. But it is possible to find out for Google, which has its own ranking method that could be seen by its toolbar that can be downloaded free and there is an area where a rank of a site from one to ten is shown. If that area is gray while visiting the site what it means is, for whatever reasons the site is in a banned list and needs avoiding in order to avoid the penalty. In addition, any link that does not have relevance to what the site is doing needs avoiding because of lack of relevancy works against the site. Keyword stuffing is a common practice and search engines do not want the repeating of keywords more than three times, as it will automatically become a spam.

Hidden text is also one of the things to avoid and how it comes into existence is if you change the text into white, it does not show on white pages, and the same could go for any text that uses the color of the background of the web page, which means the visitors to the page will not see it, but the robots will read it because what they visit is the html page. All sort of things could be hidden from view through such method to make the robot do certain things and one of them is to stuff keywords, keywords that might not be relevant to what the site is doing. If webmasters notice such an incident on their html web page they have to take measures to correct it, because if the robots find out they will penalize the site. Not to use unnecessary meta tags is also one of them and this might have to do with SEO experts or the web designers that could put a lot of it on the web page, the idea being it could be spotted by the robots by attracting their attention by highlighting a text.

Copywriting

Not everyone is doing the same thing in most cases, although there could be few similar sites doing similar things, but they cannot do it exactly the same way no matter what that being the nature of human beings or unless they are a franchise. It is those subtle differences that pay for some, of course, while others are let out into the cold, maybe not for good but for a while. If that is the case, those who stayed in the cold for a long duration should change the way they are doing business, because there is demand for almost anything scarce, which means anyone doing the right things should be able to do business. But if there is excess supply unless it dries up, doing that line of work will not be worthwhile.

If there is no excess supply and it just happened to be that it is only one webmaster that is failing to break even, what is recommended is to change the way the job is done. The key here is reaching out to customers and even if that is done through advertising, those who are visiting the site might not buy for some reason, because something might have to change. In today's surfing pattern those who are visiting a site are not always determined buyers, but they could be in need of something. Or let us assume that they have some disposable income and they do not know for sure how to use it, which means they will appreciate some help and guidance. That is when the copy of a professionally designed site will tell the undecided customer what he or she will gain by buying what the site is offering.

So having a professional site means the copy also has to be done professionally unless the webmaster has the knack and in no uncertain terms, visitors will have to be engaged in and will have to be enticed to part with their hard earned money. We have also to remember that people are impulse buyers and what they want is to see something that will give them some value for their money that they would consider it is worth it. What this means is all buyers are not resolute although some exactly know what they are looking for. How could they become resolute? Either they are repeat customers and have had the opportunity of witnessing the benefits of the products or the service or they have made research by comparing many similar products and vendors. If the site they are visiting stands out they will part with their hard-earned money. Which means the site has a lot of work to do to convenience first-time visitors to take notice of what the site is doing, and who knows that could be considered a promising start.

This issue will be touched on because many people believe that once they have a web site up and running people will buy from them. In reality it does not work like that most of the time. It is only when someone sells the necessities indulging is such a confidence is permissible, because if we talk about food items, no one buys a bag of apple or orange with an intention to use it for a whole month, not even a week. Which means that customer will come back and if not that particular customer, there are others in a big number. However, when we talk about durable goods such as computers, the buyer might have a laptop at his disposal; in fact he or she could be surfing the Internet using an older model laptop. He or she wants to buy a latest one, but there is no hurry, because the money is not going to go anywhere in most cases or the source of the payment might be through financing.

So such buyers are in a position to compare everything and take their time and except knowing that they will buy a new laptop at one point they do not know which company will sell it to them. If a given vendor gives them a niche that they will not want to pass up, just right there they will part with their money to posses some shiny laptop. Like we said it there are between 20 to 30 or even more online stores that are selling similar products, but a small niche offered by one of them with a little bit of a twist might entice a customer to make a decision.

That is what doing business on the Internet means, in fact. Anywhere else, sellers will have to wrack their brain to come up with niches that are better than competitors to close a sale, and there is no elsewhere that this will be more pronounced than on the Internet. In the brick-and-mortar case, because of inconvenience people want to do a brisk business at the first store they walk into. For the most part because of the nature of the business, they cannot find ten stores selling similar items side by side, because it is not good for business. On the Internet, it is different because that is what happens exactly.

By simply typing "online stores selling laptops" on the search engines, maybe 20 of them could pop up in a row in the search result. Which one is going the customer to choose? The top three have the best chance to be in line for doing a comparison, the main reason why everyone wants to get to the top three spots. In fact, the first spot is where everyone wants to be, because if buyers find what they want they might not go anywhere else. If they do, the first three will tell them what the market price of the product they are looking for is, and in most case buyers do not have to visit more than the first ten sites before they get what they are looking for.

Then they will have to have some niches for choosing one over the other like, for example, where the two of them are charging shipping and one of them is free, or a discount might be offered. That seller could close the sale for simply availing one nominal advantage. But the fact of the matter is sellers spy on their competitors and in order not to be outdone they will provide what the others are availing, and eventually one niche could attract buyers and that is what counts.

Like the other key components that will make a web site do what it is doing better, sales copy is very essential because it is words that would tell a visitor what is available, even if graphics have certain capability, and videos could take a notch further by combining audio and video presentation, which might not be void of words in a form of sentences. As a result, the copy of a site is very important no matter how it is presented in convincing the visitors why they should do business with a given site. It is not possible to overlook the fact that there are other competitors and in fact a visitor might have already been to a good number of sites that are doing the same thing, and could have been shopping around. So, in no uncertain terms they have to know what benefit they will get by paying for the offered product or service. That is when the copy comes in, explaining what are the particular niches the site is offering from other competitors.

What this means is visitors will have to be able to tell if not in seconds at least in the first one or two minutes what they are getting exactly and the way the site is constructed should be in such a way that they will encounter whatever they have to know on an easily accessible area, even if accessing other pages through a link is involved. One of the key functions sites should accomplish immediately when someone visits is to build confidence, because people are being duped on a daily basis and for the most part they are wary of most of the sites they are encountering. To put aside such doubt, they have at least to do one business and that is one of the reason why the first sale made to a new customer is crucial.

It will make them familiar with the payment system, which should ascertain it is very safe from the outset. A site has to display all the recognized signs that people are familiar with and other similar sites are using to ascertain the payment system is safe. Using the known financial services could be a shortcut and a guaranty, because people do not care unless there is not going to be a complication, and even if something goes wrong they know they would be covered. However, this is not going to be their immediate concern.

Say for example if a customer wants to download an ebook and if something goes wrong, such as not to be able to download the ebook in a given frame of time, the customer knows how to cancel the transaction if the problem cannot be rectified. The problem is it will take time for the money to go back to the account and if the same problem is repeated with a number of businesses, it is not only that the customer will not be able to go out and buy what is needed on time, canceling many transaction from different vendors will put the customer into a hotbed with the financial establishments, and it is these kinds of customers who have dreads to do business on the Internet. Many people talk about what happened to them and when buyers approach vendors, it is with such dreads lingering on their mind.

It is not only that, what about the goods or services themselves that they are paying for? How could they be certain that they are genuine without trying them, because still there are some bad apples out there that are ripping off many people. How many burning should people endure in order to do business on the Internet? Any business has to distinguish itself from these hordes. One way to do that is by using an effective copy, even if copy is also the most effective tool for those who are doing shoddy business too. Sometimes, keeping testimonials with photos might help a lot, because people could be afraid to attach photos with fake testimonials, but considering the number of web sites, it is unthinkable the owner of the photo will find out about it. Yet if some of the individuals that are giving the testimonial give access to be reached, it will be more than helpful, but people might not want to be bothered, and crooks could exploit that.

Therefore, it is the very first sale that will build good relation with any seller and once that has gone through without a hitch if anything happens on a repeat business it could easily and quickly be rectified. Hence, making sure that such incidents will not happen is paramount than any ad effort, because a flocking traffic could be turned off one by one for simply not encountering the right things in place.

Knowing the Search Engines

Search engines are the key for the Internet existence because they are the ones that go out and index all the material on the Internet so that it will be systematically made available to those who are seeking information in whatever form it is. That was the whole idea of search engines at the beginning, but eventually it was natural that they should evolve to become a means many people will be using to make money through, a lucrative living for some. So the whole idea is people will upload what they are doing to the Internet and through the search engines surfers who are looking for what they are offering will find them, be it a product or a service. Like it was mentioned earlier the major search engines do not require submitting sites for them although doing so might expedite the indexing process, which is very key here because it could take months if not years just to be indexed, and then to be placed in a favorable position in the search results where there are a good number of odds to beat.

One of the requirements search engines want from sites is to have some value for those who are going to visit them so that they will not be wasting their time. However, there is a paradox here like in everything else, because if a web site is doing a certain business, as long as it offers that business effectively it should not be required to add more value. Those who are visiting it will do so because of what it is offering, not because it is laden with what the search engines are calling value. That might be applicable to sites that do not sell a product or a service, because if they have to clutter the search results, they better be ready to at least offer some value for visitors that they are diverting from the selling sites. Because there are not different sections for those that are selling and for those that are providing information only in the search results. If both types meet the SEO requirements they could end up on top of search results, because both have their own kind of demand that will make it difficult to dismiss one in favor of the other. Not everyone surfing is a buyer, but most surfers are looking for information, which makes the non-selling sites important.

However, those who are selling have to know the behavior of the search engines so that they can take advantage of what they offer. The robots could come out on a daily basis to perform certain tasks and some sites will get frequent visits than others, whereas every site will at least be visited once a month, because that is the spiders' schedule. It is possible to make them visit frequently and that is done whenever there is new material, and such a visit is an update.

Google, for example, has what is known as Google Map where a user can fill out a form telling Googlebot which page on a site is changing frequently and the webmaster wants that change to be reflected on the search results quickly. What this will do is such a site will get a special treatment where Googlebot will automatically find out when there is a change and it will come out to do the updating, which will make the site current in the log of the robot. It will definitely put any site at a favorable position for search results, for the keywords that the site is using. Consequently, knowing about the existence of the Google Map and how to use it is helpful for webmasters.

It does not matter whether a site is selling or not if the search engines are asking for it, having current content is advised, and in most cases it could be in a form of articles educating visitors about what the site is doing. On the other hand, there is free content to use from numerous sites, even if when there is duplicated content the robots could find out and the end-result is penalty. It is also possible to put automated content on a site using RSS and whenever those contents are updated it will show on the site, displaying fresh content, and it will meet the requirement, but eventually if the robot finds out there is content duplication it could again penalize the site. The conclusion is even if it is going to be time consuming if the search engines want the public to be more informed about what sites are doing and if they say they will reward such sites for doing so by giving them good position on the search results it should be followed through. It is also possible to tweak a free material found on other sites so that it will look unique.

One other thing search engines do not want on a site is a dead link and if a dead link is spotted it will have to be removed quickly. Otherwise, it will take a while until the robots visit again. There is a black list such sites will go into for failing to meet certain requirements and those who know about it call it Google's SandBox. What it is, in fact, is at the beginning there is something called a waiting period before a site is included into the active list when it is indexed for the first time and that happens if there is some kind of a shortfall. It is different than an outright refusal, because there could be some sites that would not be indexed, and the search engines state that they do not include all sites when the submitting is done.

But it is difficult to say why some sites will have to wait longer before they are included in the active list except that there is something called aging, which means sites and their incoming links have to age for a certain period before they are included in the active list. Also those sites that are penalized for any reason will be kept in the Google sand Box for a while before they get a visit from the robot that will make them current that is if they are not banned.

The reason why it is like that is Google, for example, always changes its algorithms, the formula it uses to index sites and to give them rank in the search results. No one for sure knows what the algorithm is made up of except guessing and trying to outdo it. That is the main reason why the algorithms are top secret because there are webmasters that will go to any length to manipulate the algorithms to get the best spots if they know what they are.

One of the reasons that made SEO such a hot potato is this interaction where out of a sudden a site that had a good position in the search results could be dropped for some unknown reason, and the job of the SEO experts is to find out why. They will do what it takes to put back the site where it was. It is not only that they keep a very close eye on what the search engines are doing to guess what the algorithms would be, because at times it is possible to tell from what they are doing to a site what kind of formula they are using. Since they make money by showing results where they have to keep their customers' sites at the top of the search engine results if something goes wrong for good it will cost them business.

It is important because people spend a lot of money, mainly through SEO companies to get a good spot on the search result. When they out of a sudden lose that position they could panic, because it could mean like locking the front door of a store so that customers will not have access to what the store is doing. There is undoubtedly a heavy dependence on the search engines to do business over the Internet, but till date there is no other better means than that. Yet, we will touch on the other means, where some of them come close to the search engines or even better depending on who is giving the judgement, but there is a lot of work involved.

Lately, businesses have been introducing blogs and they work much better for businesses that are household names, because it is just a matter of entering the URL to go to the site or to the blog. But for other businesses since a blog is free and could be indexed like web sites where the requirements are totally different, at least, even if it is not a guaranty, it could be used as another outlet that is out there and could attract customers, because people could find out what a site is doing through the blog.

The other key advantage of blogs is that they can bring out the robots often, because if a blog is using the new phenomenon known as RSS, both major search engines have no choice other than updating those blogs or sites that are attached to My Yahoo or with other host of aggregators because whenever there is change they will come out to do their update and it does not matter how many times a day. Any site attached to such a blog if it has a link will be accessed and will always remain current and most blogs and forums are launched from web sites, which means the sites will be visited many times a day depending on how the blog or the forum is busy. So starting either a blog or a forum or if there is a site that changes its contents regularly connecting it to My Yahoo, Google, and the other aggregators will definitely make the site fresh.

The search engines have advertising systems that we will discuss as we go along, which is their breadline and either it could be expensive for some or supplementing the ad with a site that is optimized generically is very helpful. The one thing everyone likes about the Internet is anyone with a shoestring budget can try to do something and by simply using organic optimizing the same web site can compete for the same eyeballs the paying advertisers are competing for.

Marketing a Web Site

Once the web site is ready, up and running, and all what it requires generically had been put in place, whether it is indexed or not, because even if a site is not indexed it could be found by its URL, the marketing campaign could kick in. The very best place to start to get an immediate result is from pay-per-click (PPC) advertising, because in most cases the minute the formalities are in place the site could be up and running for the keywords it is registered for. What is PPC advertising? There might not be hardly anyone who has not heard about this phenomenon. But just for the benefit of the doubt, to know what PPC advertising is all about, it is good to go over the basics. It, of course, stands for pay-per-click through, which means the advertiser pays whenever visitors click through the ad the webmaster is putting with the search engines.

What is involved is the webmaster will open an account with one of the search engines Google or Yahoo. Through the opening process, the webmaster will choose keywords users would use to find the involved web site. Now, things could get a bit complicated because there are many people doing the same given line of works and when all of them approach the ad displaying services they will be asked to choose keywords. At one point, it is unavoidable that almost all of them will choose the known "hot keywords". These keywords are what searchers are using on the search engines when they look for particular goods or services. If there are 100 sellers providing the same products and services using the same keywords, which one of them will end up on the top of the list for the involved keywords? That is a difficult question to answer and it is not only that, at least which one of the sellers will be allowed the next 10 or 20 spots, those being the mostly visited ads, but the list could go on.

That is when the search engines introduced bidding on keywords. How it works is at the time of opening an account with these services the first thing the webmasters does is choosing keywords. Then the second important question is how much money are they willing to spend on advertising in a given day, where there is a minimum in most cases and it is $1. What this translates into is the advertiser will only spend a maximum of $30 a month no matter what takes place that is unless the minimum amount is higher. Then the other important question that makes a big difference is how much the webmaster is willing to pay for every click through. Click through here is when a visitor clicks through the ad that will be displayed when the chosen keywords are used by users. The advertiser will pay what he agreed to pay for each click through in spite of the visitors who clicked through buy or not. In addition, even here there is a minimum bidding amount to activate certain keywords even if the minimum allowed bid is .01.

Let us say the webmaster agrees to pay only .01 per click through and with a daily maximum ad cost of $1 the site could have up to 100 visitors. After that, because it reaches its daily maximum the site will not be on display even if users are using the chosen keywords continuously. Therefore, it is a very reasonable way of advertising and there is only one more cost added to it that is known as impression cost where if the site had been displayed 1000 times the webmaster will be charged .25, and everyone could live with such an arrangement. Even here agreeing to pay more for every 1000 impression could raise the number of impressions, but even the 1000 impressions could be overwhelming if the keywords chosen are the right ones.

If there is a catch it is when we go back to what we started about how so many advertiser could get the top spot using similar keywords. The bid they are willing to make makes the difference. The one who pays .05 for a given keyword will come ahead of the one who pays 02 for the same keyword, and if 99 of the other 100 advertisers are paying .05 the one that is paying .02 will come at the 100th rank, which might not be good for business. Among those who have agreed to pay .05 the one that will get the top spot is the one who pays .06, and if all them agreed to pay .05, most probably they will display them alphabetically, but since there are those who keep their bidding open, those will get the top spots until they are maxed out.

Therefore, at the time of choosing the keywords there is a system that will reveal how much using a given set of keywords will cost the advertiser. Most advertisers will do it according to that and in most cases, it could be expensive, but it all depends on what one is doing. Because when we see these kinds of ads displayed at the right side of the search results, they are not crowded most of the time, which means there is a good chance for anyone to be found for the keywords they choose.

It is not only that it takes to be a little bit smart at the time of choosing the keywords, because one word keywords are always expensive since those who want to bid high will use them. Therefore, the recommendation is to use two or three word phrases with the assumption that users will use such terms. It is always up to the users to decide what to do, because most bidders will leave their pay-per-click rate open so that they can always get the top spot and it will cost them .01 more than the highest bidder and since many people are using the same tactic that is why PPC becomes very expensive. Some will put a higher cap on the PPC rate so that if the bidding amount passes that limit they will go for the second or whatever position that amount will enable them to attain, but at the end there is a ceiling that the bidding cannot pass for practical reasons.

In most cases businesses that are doing similar things are victim of this kind of uncontrolled spiral cost of advertising, but the good thing about it is they cannot do it beyond what they can afford or beyond what they can offset. What will happen in the worst case scenario is the ad cost will eat into the otherwise healthy profit they would have made. That is why people choose to go with generic advertising because the cost, more or less, is predictable and if the webmasters are able to spend time on the web site they could eliminate the cost.

The reality here is the PPC advertising definitely costs money, yet making it affordable is possible and reasonable by any standard, especially when compared with the offline advertising methods that are totally out of the reach of the ordinary businesses. Here it is just a matter of visiting sites like Google that has its AdWords program and a few others like Overture of Yahoo, 7search, Kanoodle, Miva, and more that have PPC advertising whose cost can be compared. For starters, it is very cheap to start the Google AdWords ad campaign for example. All that is required is a $5 activation fee and from there on a maximum daily budget of $1.00 at the rate .01 could bring your site in front of buyers that are asking what your site is doing.

The trick is in the keywords that are used, because like it was mentioned earlier those that are known as "hot keywords" are being used by many sellers that are selling the same products and services a webmaster could be selling. What that means is those who pay more for those keywords will come on top of the ads displayed, and it is done in most cases at a high cost depending on the line of work. If you want to sell real estate online, get prepared for the plucking, because the bidding war could go through the roof.

If one seller agrees to pay any amount to always hold the first spot on the displayed ads for a given keyword, such an advertiser can always keep the top spot, and the bidding is done automatically. All the advertiser has to do is, after doing a good research that could be done on the site about what will be the highest bid, keep an open bidding system, and the system itself will give the advertiser the top spot for the highest bid plus .01. This means if someone had agreed to pay $100 for the top spot and gets a click through it will cost him that if the other bidders are bidding that high. But if the highest bid is only $10 the advertiser that agreed to pay $100 will have to pay only $10.01 if someone clicks through the ad, where the higher bid is just a safety mechanism not to lose the top spot. However, there is the impression payment only for getting the top spot on regular basis. Someone has to click on the ad to pay the agreed upon sum, and the payment will be effected regardless of whether there was a transaction or not.

What this shows is there might not be a need to bid unless what is being done warrants it where, for example, someone who sells a $300,000 item like real estate bids $10 for every click through and if the 100th click through closed the transaction the cost involved will be $1000 for advertising, which might not be high. But for someone selling a one-time item of $3000 such as a used car if the sellers agrees to pay $10 for every click through and the 100th click bought the car, the sellers will lose one-third of the price and it will be unreasonable. All in all, when we compare PPC with generic marketing, it is possible that it could beat the chase for even paying .01 per click depending on the kind of keywords chosen. For the most part that is why people are saying not to go for the "hot keywords" that are mostly made up of one word, but opt for phrases. There is software that will generate a big number of keywords to choose from.

Most of the PPC advertising systems have help with choosing the right keywords for the intended products and there is a certain bidding price attached to it from past experience so that it is possible to arrive at a given estimate for a given month. That is a good reminder of how much could be incurred, but certainly it is not an exact figure, and it is possible to overrun it by simply choosing one's own daily maximum budget and cost of the per click. It is also good to start at a lower price and see what the outcome will be and then raising it is always possible if it is not effective. Conclusion, if there is a good advertising system that will get an immediate result with the unheard amount of $1.00 maximum limit and .01 per click through it is PPC advertising.

After reaching the maximum amount, the ad will be off for the day, which means it will not be on display. With the above arrangement, if middle-of-the-road keywords are chosen, it will mean 100 clicks, and if all those clicks are being exhausted on a daily basis hiking it up to $2 or more is not going to harm, because from 100 visitors at least between five and six could be buyers. If doubling the number of visitors means 10 –12 buyers it means it is worth an extra $1.00 which will easily be recovered from the extra sales, and it could go on, the minimum arrangement being this.

The problem is if there are many people bidding using the same keywords it might be difficult to get the top spots. Statistics has it that people do not shop around if they get what they want at the beginning of the lineup, so that there might arise the need to hike the amount forked out. The truth of the matter is people are doing good business because these kinds of visitors are as good as qualified buyers. For the most part, they are definitely after what is on offer, and it all depends on what kinds of niches capture their attention

In addition it helps to know what is taking place in the world of advertisement, where there is only one recent arrival and, which is taking a good bite out of the total of $1.85 trillion that is 7 percent of the total sales of $28 trillion in the U.S. according to Direct Marketing Association by the simple advertising method known as PPC. The recent arrival, the Internet marketing gets $284 billion of the total sales getting ahead of newspapers ad of $213 billion and DRTV's of $150 billion. The number one undisputed medium is non-catalog direct mail sales, which amounted to $483 billion followed by telephone marketing $402 billion.

What could be read from this is the Internet marketing will close the existing gap within the coming few years with a projected percentile growth of 12.6 percent followed by radio of 7.5 percent and TV and magazine advertising of 6.4 percent. When seen from the perspective of buyers, one of the main reasons cited for putting the blimp behind Internet marketing is the real time buying phenomenon that is unmatched by the other mentioned mediums except telephone marketing, which can close a deal immediately. Nonetheless, buyers could get their lead from print media like magazines and newspapers or from watching TV or listening to the radio. Then they will have to take a mind note either to visit the store or the web site.

The reason why Internet buying is on the rise is, traditionally there had always been two approaches toward sales, where either the buyers will have to be approached directly, cold-calling, or direct marketing techniques like direct mail, indirectly through ad display or buyers go out and search for what they are looking for. There had never been a medium that combined both with a relative ease. It avails a huge number of choices, offers, comparison of prices, verification of quality of products, even delivery, as there are digital products that are easy to download immediately. Hence, it is not surprising if the Internet is gaining on the traditional mediums, which are becoming more of a cold medium.

It does not mean there is no room for innovation among the old mediums, but that innovation will have to be introduced through technology, which is giving the leg-up to the Internet, because the possibilities are unlimited. The genre of the advertising method of the Internet is on the rise, whereas the other mediums have a lot to do in that respect.

The Internet started out with email marketing that had to grow hand-in-hand with the number of the Internet users, which would have been a painful growth if there were not an explosion in the number of the Web surfers.

Email got enhancing from text and banner ads that did not only revolutionize the Internet marketing, but snatched a lot of business from the traditional mediums. Then search came into the picture that is not different from going out and shopping except that it availed a lot of variety, possibilities, and convenience under one roof, through one medium when compared with catalog sales, for example, that has no choice other than to be very much limited with what it can offer. Once there is a build up of constant visitors flocking to the various search engines, a paid search was introduced so that those who can pay could get the cream of the crop, and the unbeatable powerful engine of the Internet till date had come into existence with it.

Lately, video advertising had been introduced and it is adding to the genre since it is better situated in presenting products and services than text and the static banner ads to capture the attention of buyers, within the split seconds that ads have to do the trick in presenting what is up for grab. In this particular area, ads on prints like newspapers or inserts that could take a whole page could present to visitors more in one quick glance. Yet, they do not come near web sites with their rich resources and they are always a click away for those who want to know more about a product or a service, once their ads are encountered by those who are conducting search and they can do business in real time unlike most of the mediums.

If there is anything touted to wrestle back this new attained customer allure from the Internet, it is interactive TV, which is said to be on the making to avail more possibilities for the viewers than the passive flipping through the numerous channels. Viewers could have a lot of access depending on how much and how fast the technology is developed, and what it is going to mean is bundling TV viewing and Internet surfing together, which will definitely bring back what direct marketing through TV had lost. People can do everything that they are doing on the Internet by using computers, this time by simply using their specially equipped TV sets and their remote control, which is going to be buying right off the TV ad. Which one will be a more enjoyable medium remains to be seen.

When we see it from the point of view of advertisers, most probably Internet has evolved beyond anyone's speculation, because it is driving traffic in a big number for many businesses who would have still stayed in the yellow pages and the classified section of print media, as the rest of advertising mediums were not attainable because of the high advertising cost involved.

But now, even if the bidding could raise the mark if keywords are chosen carefully, the Internet is affordable. It is not only that advertisers might not have to spend a dime if they have the time, or a very reasonable amount if they want to go the generic way, which could avail the same opportunity of being found by paying search to a certain extent. However, the pay search for sure will avail a sure shortcut and a huge break for those who had been paying a lot to advertise on the various expensive mediums such as TV, newspaper, magazine, and radio.

That being said if there is one thing discomforting, the line is blurring between getting a big share of the ad money and doing the job. An ad on a yellow page or on a classified section of a local newspaper has more visibility because everyone who goes through the classified section will see it, and the same applies with everyone who picks the yellow pages. Whereas, because of how the number of the impressions are working on Internet advertising, and because of the lack of matching between the keywords businesses choose and buyers use, even the highest bidding businesses could lose customers, and the statistics is not coming clearly yet on where businesses are getting their most business from, since it is a known reality that when it comes to advertising, most businesses mix mediums.

The conclusion is the new arrival on the ad scene will eventually get away with the big chunk of the ad money and most of the traditional mediums cannot do much to deter it except withering away by changing their form. They might have to take the plunge into the Internet, as people are using it, more and more, to obtain their information too, and almost all popular publications have their Web presence, yet what they generate in a form of ad is miniscule for the most part. The good news is the print media still has its readership even if its ad share had been eroded and it is not in an immediate danger of being extinct.

Radio is riding the storm because people have to move from place to place, whether they are biking, hiking, driving, even flying, and more. Radio is the only medium that could accompany them, even while they are doing things, which sends a signal to advertisers that they can have access to many people through this particular medium, and they will be willing to pay.

For users the new technology makes their life easier, while at the same time it makes advertising cheaper for businesses even if the cost is slowly creeping up, and unless it is backed with result the anxiety could subside and things could go back to the old way of doing things.

Good Sales Pitch and the Rest of Them

Good copy, a professionally made web site, no cluttering so that searchers will get what they want with a minimum effort, because most Internet buyers have time constraints, should part every ad campaign. Good reasonable niches will also have to be in place to outdo other competitors and to close the sale. Most sellers spy on what their competitors are doing and there is nothing wrong in doing that, since the intent is to offer a better service than them so that they will not outdo them, and this kind of competition will not only bring the best out of everyone but rewards the one that has the best offer. As we know it that is how price is checked, because anyone charging an exorbitant price will be asking the visitors to vote with their foot, forcing them to flock to where the price is reasonable. When there are a big number of suppliers of the same service and product obviously there will be a checking mechanism where there might not be enough market for everyone selling the given product and service. Some will have to go under or change their form, because what they are doing is not going to be profitable.

Yet, since doing business on the Internet, including the ads is affordable, many people can go on doing it for a long period of time, or if it is an offshoot of a brick-and-mortar it will easily pay the bills and the online venture eventually might cover its cost and show some result. Because if we see what is happening today, almost everyone needs a phone line without thinking of doing anything on the Internet, and adding around $10 on that is not going to cause a damage on a budget. All in all, a profitable business could be run within a targeted budget range of $1000 or less, and if it is profitable, it means it will cover its cost. If it does not that is what it will cost for a given number of months until the business is profitable and as we know it when people go into business, they always have a huge war-chest, which shows what they will incur might not even be considered an expense. They could spend more than that for entertainment in one month, so have a profitable business!

The other effective advertising method is email marketing because the potential is even huge as it can reach a big number of would be prospects. In fact, it is cold calling for the most part, and there are several ways to go about doing it. There are companies that will charge a fee for sending out ads on behalf of webmasters depending on how much money they are willing to pay, because the fee goes up according to the number of email sent out, and we are talking a ceiling of millions of emails. These companies have access to a big number of list and how they get their hand on the list vary from business to business, but saying that there are businesses that are selling list will suffice here, because they could harvest their own list or they could buy the list. However, there is no guarantee that those who will receive the email ad have agreed to receive the ad, except that they will be given the opportunity to opt out if they do not like it and it is the job of the company to do the follow up if it is another company that is sending out the ads.

The business of harvesting email accounts is doable over the Internet without the consent of the email owner and it is possible to do it both manually and automatically through software that sniffs email accounts, which is not difficult. There might not be anyone who is doing it manually, but the possibility is there, because almost every web site on search results displays an email address to be used for contacting the site owner, whether it is a business or a personal web site, and that is what a list is made up of. At the same time there are agencies, whatever they are doing enables them to gather a big number of email addresses and those kind of agencies could sell those ready made email addresses for buyers without the consent of the owners, and it had been around for a long time and it is a source of good income.

Those who are receiving the emails are not different from those prospects that are being visited in person by traditional sales people or contacted through a telemarketing campaign and what takes place is cold-calling where the targeted individual will have the option to participate in what is offered or can refuse it outright. Here also it is the same and it is not new hearing webmasters moaning about receiving a big number of junk email that are flooding their email incoming box. That is why almost all email services have the means of sifting through the incoming email and separate those mostly that are generated and sent out by software and have certain terms in them as junk mail and will make it easy for webmasters to get rid of them by simply pressing a delete button.

However, even if most of it is totally unrelated junk, there will come a time when a webmaster as a business person might want to reach a big number of prospects to promote a new or an existing business. And such effort, whether it is sent by the webmaster or a hired company, whether it is done manually or automatically (sending millions of emails manually is not practical) will be labeled as a junk mail and be sent to the thrash bin with one click, because people really get tired of going through these huge barrage of advertising that offers little for the most part. But here we have to be reasonable because almost all junk mails are some kind business proposal and it might not offer something for everyone it is sent out to, but those who are engaged in such an advertising method are known to make money, which means there are people that go through some of them if not all of them.

There is no means of making the prospects open the email except using eye-catching and impressive short messages, even then for those of us who experience these barrage of messages, because they are overwhelming it is not possible to go over all of them, but some of them could be read. It is not only that some of them can escape the filter of the email service providers and could enter the incoming mail and they might get chance to be viewed. Even if they are a good means of reaching many prospects theoretically, especially when seen from the number that is being sent out, but that could end up being labeled as junk email no matter what useful message they could be carrying, it is doubtful to say they are useful because they end being deleted in a big bulk, yet the statistics says such advertisers make a lot of money.

Nevertheless, when they are applied in most cases it will be a onetime arrangement where a given number of email holders who could be doing anything will receive a convincing ad telling them to do what the advertiser want them to do, and if they are interested they will follow through. By simply clicking a link, they can land on the advertiser's site. From there on they could become prospects or not. Some might cancel it the first time, while some might let the ad come again and again, although that happens only if the site owners are sending out the ad, because it is not going to cost them, assuming that they are using a software that is capable of sending out millions of ads. That is how everyone is doing it now, and no one can send out millions of ads using the manual method, because the individual will become old without even sending out a mere 100,000 emails.

As result, the chance of being reported as spammers exists in the course of trying to reach prospects, only if the site owners keep on sending out the same ad, especially after the recipient had made it clear not to receive any more of the ads through the mandatory opt-out clause that should be included to enable recipients to stop these incoming emails. As a webmaster, if you are using one of this software, make sure you include the opt-out clause because it is required by law, and once you received the opt-out email the particular email address should be removed from the list.

But here again, almost all of these efforts that will be labeled as junk email when they reach the other end might not even get a chance of being opened because of the above mentioned reason and could be shown into the garbage bin with a click of a button, resulting the chance of being labeled as spammers is slim. But some people might read the emails that is if say for example the email address is new and in that case it could take a while until that critical point is reached where they will want to opt-out. We all have had that experience or even there might be some that could be looking for something that might go through all their email they receive and they could end up being prospects.

No matter what, now we know it could be done by webmasters themselves who will have to buy the software which is not more than $50 for the most part, or they might have to pay a fee, which could eventually surpass the cost of the software. There are more expensive software with more bell and whistles as there are services that charge more since they could offer more service like a repeat send-out, where it is possible to pay for a given number of send-outs for a given number of months or for a year.

What is key here is the only thing generated from such a campaign is just traffic and the web site with its effective design and copy will have to convert these visitors into buyers. The chance could go either ways, because selling is easy once the decision is made on the part of the buyer, but marketing is a difficult task that can only be measured by the amount of success it avails in parallel to the cost incurred. That is why marketers should also know their budget in advance and if they overshoot more than a targeted budget what they are going to realize after they close the sale is the effort is not going to be their worthwhile.

Another similar way of attracting visitors with the hope of converting them into buyers is using a newsletter where visitors are asked to sign in to receive the newsletter at a given interval and as opt-ins the chance of converting them into buyers is high. In addition, the newsletter also should focus to a good extent on what the business is doing while being informative in the chosen endeavor. The one issue here is the subscribers are giving out their email address willingly, which means they are open for anything as long as they know where it originates from. They should not be limited to the newsletter only. It is possible to direct other promotional material into their email address with the option to opt-out included in the offer.

The newsletter could also be used to educate or inform them about what the business is doing, about its future plans, including who its competitions are, the state into which the business is in, and the like so that, eventually, some kind of a follow up and loyal customer base could be created in accordance to what the business is offering. This kind of email address could be valuable and if it is not abused those who are participating are as good as prospects who will be kept tuned in into what goes on and when the right time comes they could do business with the site.

We have touched on reciprocal links in relation to optimizing a site for the search engine indexing and the ongoing good ranking of the web site in search results. Reciprocal links can also be built keeping in mind that they will be another source of traffic, which could get better when it is done with alike web sites, but by no means with competing web sites that are doing the exact similar things. Depending on what one is doing it is possible to find sites that are doing complementary things and every item sold or service given has these kinds of sites. If a site is selling books online there are tons of sites that fall into this category and it does not matter if they are selling books, even if it is similar to one the site is selling. They might have a big number of visitors, because for some reason, whatever the offer is on a given web site it could attract their attention. There are publishing houses that could carry thousands of books, but if they allow reciprocal link, it will mean as good as being included in their index list except that the advertising site is making its own sale.

There are hundreds of indexes that are doing so many things that ask surfers to include their business and including the URL of a site in these indexes will increase the exposure of a site, and search engines might consider that an incoming link. There are indexes and directories that deal with a big number of items, but they always have a special section for what a particular site is doing, and when people visit those sites looking for exactly what a site could be doing, the chance to be found is always there and what the site is doing to beat competitors is what makes the difference. Always the copy and the professional look of a site will make the buyers feel they are dealing with a site that knows its stuff or knows what it is doing or is among the authorities in what is being done.

There are many ways of creating such impressions and one of them is by displaying pictures, which could tell people what kind of people are running the site. If the picture is the owner's, even the better, because even if buyers do not care about who is exactly running a site as long as they find what they need, some might want to be personal, and thank the owner for giving a good service, which could result in confidence building. Next time if something goes wrong, at least there is someone who would carry the brunt and someone to reproach to correct the mistake instead of the impersonal support team, even if that is not the case in almost all cases, because business people always do care for their customers, since that is the nature of things. They depend on their customers to do business as their customers depend on them to give them good service as well as products.

One other thing that is highly recommended is to write articles or have them written by someone and submit them to ezines that have a big network as there are a good number of them around. They display the articles on many web sites that have a reasonably good traffic and the chance of diverting some of that traffic is there. It is not only that if the articles are about what the site is doing, disseminating a lot of information about the business is possible, or else what it takes is to be a little bit creative to make those who are reading the articles to visit the site and eventually they could be converted into buyers.

Advertising on offline publications even if the expense is not affordable is highly recommended, but that might not be the preferred way to go for a small business that is trying to see a business take off the ground with a shoestring budget. Nevertheless, there are many means of telling others what an entrepreneur is doing. We do not have to forget that the offline marketing has had its own regiments of advertising methods all along that starts form business cards, brochures, to catalogs, calendars, mugs, T-shirts, pens with the logo of the company, and so on. Even company stationery can be made to carry the URL of the business. Cars also are great because the URL can be plastered with the name of the company somewhere it is very visible and the business does not even have to have a brick-and-mortar business.

Affiliate marketing is one of the known ways of advertising a web site, about what a business or a site is doing, once a way of inviting and recruiting affiliates is in place. After that, it is the affiliates themselves that will promote the business for the commission they make whenever their effort brings in buyers. All they need is to have a means of advertising the businesses, which is usually done with a text or banner ad that could be displayed on the affiliates' web site despite what they are doing, and whenever a prospect buys by clicking through a particular banner displayed on a particular web site, the site owner will get a commission according to the arrangement. Mostly what attracts affiliates is the commission paid out and some track record about the site. A verifiable testimonial from earlier affiliates will do the job, as the whole arrangement is trust-based. If the number of affiliates who have positive feedback about a given business or web site is high, its chance of attracting a big number of affiliates will also be high.

Affiliate program is a little bit different because the affiliates will make it a priority to promote their own site so that it will have a sustainable traffic. At times the affiliates could even go as far as building an independent web site just to promote a given lucrative client whose product and service has demand and every sale that was directed through such sites will get the commission from the seller of the product or services. That is why it is recommended to have a well functioning and compensating affiliate program to go hand-in-hand with the business.

Blog also has become an important part of a web site doing business simply because any kind of material about what the site is doing could be put on the blog and there is a real time interaction where the site can gather feedback about what it is doing and what the prospects think about what is offered. Chat room also could have a similar effect although it could be a bit expensive because if it requires immediate interacting for as long as the chat is required to be on, unless the chat is directed to be among users, a moderator answering questions every now and then has to be three. If the chat is allowed to be on for 24 hours and it is between users there is no problem, otherwise that will be translated into three shifts of a reasonable well-paying job and it is only big companies that can afford that kind of an arrangement.

Blog, on the other hand, is manageable by the webmaster no matter how many times posting a reply or new material is required. Some blog sites run by big businesses have a full time staff to post interesting material about what the site is doing and to interact with the aftermath of the posting. There are also companies that will hire bloggers known as boosters who will be paid by the number of threads they post and that is a good way of creating activity. But when it comes to marketing the business, it is a much better tool than the static site where for the most part visitors can only do a few things, among them, sending email or making a phone call if they have more questions to ask about what is offered.

With the arrival of RSS, blogs can reach a big number of subscribers without costing the webmaster any money. All it takes is to register the blog to a given number of aggregator indexes, which will update every change made on the blog by the hour. And anyone who is interested to know about any changes made on the blog has to do is to register with aggregators and they will update their account with the up to the minute information of what is happening on the sites that they are registered with and all it takes is to log into their account and check which of the accounts they are registered with have new changes. A site that makes frequent changes also can make the site available for the aggregators by simply putting the RSS or the XML button on any site, and if any site or visitor wants to be informed whenever a change is made on the site all they have to do is to add it to their aggregator list they are registered with and any change will reflect there. My Yahoo, and a few handful of aggregators give a very superb free service.

Banner and text ads are among many ways a site can promote itself online and they were the pioneers of online advertising. It always had been that those who are willing and interested to display such a banner would create a source of traffic for their site. Such arrangement can be availed for a fee or free. There are a big number of sites that will carry a text or a banner ad on their site for a fee and they promote their own site aggressively so that they could attract visitors that will click on those ads, because that is how they get money from advertising and they need visitors in big number. Yet, it is difficult to measure the kind of effective service these kinds of agencies are giving for the advertisers. Although advertisers could do more than seeing their ad because they can track where each visitor is coming from if they want to because the technology is available. Those who do not use such technology could visit those who have signed up as advertisers and can check if their ad is displayed on their site and they might ask the sites to put counters. Sometimes, when someone does business with a given web site they ask how they found the particular site they are doing business with and the idea behind the asking among many others could be to find out who is directing traffic to their site.

If the site gives any kind of free service a good number of people are using, introducing banner and text ads could go a long way, and all it takes is to ask those who are using the free service to put the ad on their site. Whether the site has a big number of visitors or not, at least the banner and the text ad will be there for anyone to click on them. Some sites make the arrangement voluntary, whereas some makes it compulsory. One service to provide free is to have a free web site submitting service on a site and while people use that service they could be asked to put the banner or text ad on the web site they are submitting and could be made voluntary or compulsory.

Now things are changing fast because of the fast connection that is available with DNS and cable that have made video viewing possible. This means the number of businesses that are putting video ads on their site is on the rise, because video could give a better presentation than text or banner. When there is both video and audio, it is more involving than the static banner and text ads. At the same time so many important information about the business could be crammed into a video, which could give an experience that matches as being at the place of business in real time, and it is proven to have a much more convincing power than banners, as well as text ads alone.

Again because of the advancement of the technology where different kinds of hand-held devices are in big use today including PDAs, cell phones, and iPods, what is known as podcasting is sweeping the ad scene where short video or audio ads that could be downloaded quickly on these devices and be viewed on the go have become one lucrative way of advertising that should be included in today ad campaign to be successful. It is also possible to view these ads on laptops and desktop computers and are becoming much more effective than TV ads, yet they are not very expensive, and are affordable for most businesses.

As a result, there are numerous ways of marketing an Internet business, both offline and online, and what will draw the line is the profitability of the business, where a given amount of marketing effort should be flanked with a given amount of sales so that the cost could be offset and the next campaign kicks in. But if the first one does not show any result, what will happen is the entrepreneur or the webmaster could draw a line and says I can afford to spend this much to promote my business, but to continue to do so, at some point I have to realize this amount of profit. Because people do not advertise for fun, they want to see results, otherwise it is like throwing away money and the original resource could dry up, or as the economists say it there has to be something to be given up in order to sink money into a venture, which could be anything. As long as what is going to be given up is a complementary need, the effect could be cushioned, but the minute that line is trespassed and basic needs are going to be compromised in any way, the effort should come to a halt and scrapped, because every undertaking cannot succeed as there are some that will have to be put on the backburner for good or for a better time.

One other important issue about marketing is there is a set of standard that needs to be followed. What that means is an ad campaign that runs the whole gamut at a given interval of time is much better than the one that wants to engage with one kind of advertising only at a time, because the effect could be less. The natural steps to follow, more or less, are as they are presented here. First comes taking care of the web site making it ready for the search engines, which by itself takes a while. From the inception, to come up with the right design, which the webmaster could undertake or a professional web designer could do, all the involved work consumes time.

Then will come the SEO, which could be done by the web developers by simply keeping in mind the importance of SEO while designing the site. The webmaster could do it as well or it requires to hire SEO companies, because it takes a lot of time even if the knowledge could be acquired by doing some research, which by itself takes time, and at the end of the day it might not be as good as the one done professionally. If we think of SEO as being an ongoing effort for as long as the site is doing business, we might have to think twice, because it is going to be costly. However, the frugal way to go is at least to have the preliminary stage in place so that the search engines will index the web site. Then the question to ask is, is a webmaster planning to beat the competition with generic SEO only? If it is so either it has to be done in house, or like it was said the webmaster has to be ready to fork out some money on an ongoing basis and that will depend on the outcomes attained, but it is found to be a nerve wracking way of doing business, yet for some it might work.

Then once all the expense is incurred, let us assume there is enough traffic finding its way to the site at this early stage, and if the copy of the site is not made well, the power of converting the visitors into buyers could be compromised. That is another hole burning in the pocket. Even if it is a onetime expense, copies also go stale, but it is difficult to say how fast, yet it could be much sooner than a design. So, at least the copy also can be done by the webmaster, and if that is the case it could be updated as many times as it is found to be necessary, otherwise it could be a drain on the resources.

At this point, at least if the SEO is done well and all the requirement the search engines are looking for are there, thanks not all of the search engines are fussy, the chance of the site being indexed is there and that process can be expedited by submitting the sites. Here also the submitting could be done professionally either for one-time or with a monthly follow up for a year that being most of the arrangement. Or if the webmaster has the time it could be done in-house, because there are sites that have made the submitting process a snap and then doing it again and again on a monthly basis is not difficult. It might take a few hours every month, not a big deal really.

Like it was mentioned earlier if a blog is added it is like dragging the search engines to visit on a daily basis that is if not on hourly basis, and that will add for the freshness of the site that will translate into good position in the search results. If a site has all these requirements and if it mixes it with the paid ad, with any preferred mode, unless there is something wrong with what the web site is doing, it will be among the frequently visited sites in its category, and it also should do a good business.

One thing we have not touched on up to this point is AdSense, which is offered by Google and Yahoo also has another one known as Yahoo Publisher. What both do is if a site has a given number of visitor in a day, they will put ad on such web sites and if anyone visits the site by clicking through those ads the webmaster will be paid some amount of money that Google or Yahoo only know how to calculate. But it will be a portion of what they are making on every click through. Remember, we have said that whether there is sales or not, advertisers pay for every click through, and that is the money they will share, because if that web site was not in existence doing whatever it is doing they would have not made any money, which is a fair deal.

As a result, there are a big number of web sites and blogs that are making money this way and it has become lucrative for those that have managed to drive a huge amount of traffic to their site. This means selling a product or giving service is being complimented by advertisers who pay the search engines like it was mentioned when someone clicks on their ad, whether the click through resulted in buying or not, and that is the money the search engines are sharing with web sites that have managed to put the ads on their site and generating traffic for the advertisers, and it is a huge success story for everyone involved.

Because these ads used to be displayed only on the search engines with the search results when surfers come to use the search engines to find what they are looking for. Now the number of sites that are displaying the ads have become huge and because of the size it has become profitable both for Google that is willing to share what the advertisers are willing to pay, because do not forget we have said they bid and the amount could go through the roof.

There are also search results where the Google search button could be installed on a web site and if visitors use the search there will be ads popping up according to what is searched, otherwise it is the content of the site that will trigger the ads, one of the reasons why search engines like Google want a lot of content on web sites. The reason they want them fresh is the ads that are popping up will not be stale. All in all, this arrangement has become a good source of income for businesses that might not sell much, but could attract visitors. There are also a good number of mini web sites that are coming into existence just to do these ads and it is not surprising. People were becoming affiliates and now using their site to display ads does not take much, yet as long as they have visitors it could be more lucrative.

One thing to remember here is what triggers the search results is what is happening on the involved web sites and it has a direct relevance with what the site is doing, more than the content, yet the content also plays an effective supplementary role. In other words, the ads could be triggered by the keywords the searchers used to make it to the site. In most cases, they go with the theme or with what a site is doing. If a site is selling shoes, most definitely the ads displayed will have to do with shoes, because who is targeted here is the surfer who made it to the site using a given number of keywords that have to do with shoes. At times there are ads triggered from the content that is on the site. Consequently, there is no a guaranteed way of saying such and such site will trigger such and such ads.

We have talked about keeping fresh content on a web site will make the robots come back frequently to update their log as well as the content of the web site so that those change will be reflected on the search results. If they do not do that, they could do a disservice to the site, although saying that in no uncertain terms is difficult. But one thing for sure is as long as the old material is on the site there is no reason why the site will lose whatever position it attained using the particular material. Yet, the fresh content could give it a new edge, because whatever material that is new could play in favor of the site when the search results show up. What counts most could be the date showing the latest activity and that is common sense, but the catch is the robots keep record of a site and will compare the material.

That is why blogs with big participants make a lot of money from this because they could have a big number of visitors that are participating on the blog and whatever material they post is unique. It is not only that blog participants are frequent visitors, visiting the blog a number of times a day non-stop, for an indefinite period. Whenever they are back they will be greeted with different AdSense ad enticing them to click, and that will be translated into a lot of money for the blog moderator, and it works naturally, without no gimmick added.

Visualizing the Business

At one point, after what it takes to make an effective business online had been followed through thoroughly, it is important to detach oneself from what is implemented and look at the business, because, most probably that is how what is missing or what new changes need to be applied could be visualized. If listening to a hoard of SEO experts makes a difference, one thing they will tell their customers is to be patient if they want to take the generic way because things do not happen overnight. In addition, nothing stays the same for a long period neither. One known fact also is there are two kinds of hat wearers in the world of SEO, black hats and white hats.

The black hats will go to any length to see the sites they are in charge of finish on top of the search results and for them not exploiting any weakness in the search engines is as good as doing a disservice to those who are paying them to put their site at the top of the search results. The white hats, on the other hand, have a mode of conduct and ethics to follow. They would prefer to play ball with the search engines and for the most part are ready to exploit loopholes created, from time to time by the search engines. Their way of doing business is conservative and safe for their customers, albeit it might not show a robust result, whereas the black hats are very aggressive and could show a terrific result in a short period of time, but they could end up having the site they are working on penalized if they are caught in the act of doing wrong or spurious or dubious things according to the take of the search engines.

Consequently, the war is between the black hats and the search engines, because the search engines do not want anyone to take advantage of weaknesses they introduce into the system, form time to time. It happens no matter how careful they are and the fact that there is someone in the wing waiting for those weaknesses to happen aggravates things for them. They could lose the confidence of their paying advertisers if not the free users if they find out that some free-lodgers are getting away by doing better business than those who are parting with their hard earned money in order to do a better business than their competitors. To make things worse it is the search engines themselves that are introducing the weaknesses, it is always unknowingly, and it has to do with the nature of the coding itself where it could be difficult to spot certain mistakes in advance unless something happens, like someone taking advantage of vulnerabilities to be benefited wrongly.

Especially, a major search engine like Google has what it calls algorithms and they are just a set of rules it uses so that everyone will have a plain level field without anyone hijacking the system, and everything it does with the algorithms is top secret. Likewise, both camps the black hats and the white hats are watching eagerly what the algorithms introduce whenever it does its dance known as "Google Dance", for example.

What Google dance is the robot will go out and do indexing based on new algorithms that will be introduced from to time, or it will change a few rules, here and there, on how to conduct the searching process, without telling anyone what it is doing for the most part. But at times those who are in charge will give a press release or will do an interview saying what the new changes are or what they are expecting from webmasters or SEO experts for the foreseeable future, because nothing stays stationary for a long period of time. As a result, there is a constant war going between the three of them. The black hats could have aggressive clients who want the top spot and if they are penalized in the process, it is just a matter of starting over, but if they make it to the top level it does not matter how, all they are looking at might be to get certain benefit for as long as it could be had.

The white hats will have to fight the black hats, because their clients are not going to get the top spot as long as they are manipulating the show, and they are the ones in most cases who alert the search engines on their wake. Because of this it is easy for webmasters to tune into what is going on since there are a lot of publications, blogs, and forums that are talking about what is going on in the world of SEO, which means there is nothing done behind a closed door for a long time. The webmasters can also take measures to improve their stand in the search results without requiring help from SEO experts. They could save money as well while at the same time doing what is required for generic search results, but it might fall short of what the pros are doing, because no matter what, they do not disclose most of the techniques they are using for the most part. But at times some of them might write a book about it or might make some of the techniques public knowledge since they are all over the blogs or forums sharing ideas and anyone can sneak on what they are doing even if they do not touch technicalities often.

This shows, just making it in front of the buyers without giving too much attention to the outcome of what is being done by itself takes a lot of energy, resources, and time. It is a known fact that there is a breathtaking shortcut if it were not expensive for the most part, especially for those who are doing very similar businesses that are common place. For not simply paying the going rate of the bidding war that takes place in what some search engines are offering for whatever reasons, the one who is willing to pay the highest bid will walk away with their business. It is not difficult to see the fine line here. Take a bold measure and risk to advertise aggressively and reap the benefit that is if it is prevalent, because everyone is aiming at the same end-result and doing it with the same determination.

At the time of writing this booklet, there was a war that might give the webmasters a peek into what is happening it the bidding war. Big companies such as Mazda and Pontiac were bidding each other to death. What was happening was Mazda started bidding on the keywords Pontiac was using, which means even if they might put a cap on it if the bid is going to be open you can imagine what will happen with such heavyweights. Just to block the Pontiac ad from being displayed Mazda could spend a big amount of money and it could divert all visitors that are using those keywords to its site, and like we have mentioned it if everything is in place Mazda could steal big business from Pontiac in the open by being aggressive and pervasive.

Talking about everything being in place; what we are talking about here is the copy and maybe some niches in a form of a rebate or a discount. Because both product lines are known for their quality products, which could mean most buyers might have already made up their mind which one to buy, yet there is still a chance of swaying undecided buyers to one's side, because what buyers are looking for is known for the most part and if everything is in place who would not want to save several thousand dollars as long as they know the product they are getting is, more or less, similar except the brand name.

If buyers are into brand loyalty there is nothing anyone of the sellers could do to convert such customers for the short haul, but for the long haul, it is possible to attract this group. But if what they are looking for is value, anyone of them who wins the bid if they have what exactly the buyers are looking for, they got their business, otherwise buyers will definitely search for other vendors that will render them the value they are looking for. If visitors do not know the existence of what Pontiac is offering, but because of the bidding war they might have encountered the Mazda offer, and somehow if they like what they see, they will walk away with the Mazda offer. But if not, they will search for someone else that will offer them the value they are looking for, but it might not be Pontiac because it was shortcut by the measure Mazda took, which shows why some people cling to the generic marketing, since they might not know which one of their competitors would hit them and block their bidding.

Even if a bid could be open, at one point there has to be a cap to it, because for selling a $10,000 product, in the mindset of every seller there is a limit that they cannot surpass. Yet, when you take the above mentioned car companies, since they have a huge advertising budget and they make their money by mass selling, they could spend millions of dollars on bidding war. But for the smaller competitors what is required is passing the cap with a few margins and they will end up closing the sale between them leaving someone out in the cold. If there is a web site that is making it in the search results with a good position using only generic SEO, its chance of doing business will not be snatched. Here also it is possible to be outdone because a competitor, in fact can copy the generically prepared web site and improve on it making the other one bite the dust, and that is why competitors are keeping an eye on what each other are doing and when they know what measure the others are taking, to outdo them they up the ante.

For the most part there is a software that can disclose what a site is doing, what kind of keyword it is using, what kind of links it has, the kind of SEO method it is using by simply typing the keywords the particular webmaster is using into the software and clicking a button. That is why keeping an eye on a competitor's site has a payoff and most probably that is what SEO companies are doing for their customers. They simply spot who their major competitor of a given client are and do a much better optimization, and the search engines give the better rank for the site that is done better.

All it takes for a competitor to know what a web site is made up of without even using a software is by clicking "view" on IE toolbar and from the dropdown menu click on "source", and what is seen in there is what makes up a given site, doing the same thing to another web site could put the other site on the top spot this well done site is enjoying. There is no reason why that site's copy, optimization, links and other elements that are making it finish ahead cannot be copied, but not word for word, and on the top of that all it takes is to add new things to even make the other site better. That is where most SEO companies are making a killing.

This will bring us back to the point where even if going it alone through the advertising route might seem to cut through the chase, it will not do it for every business, especially those that are doing similar businesses. If someone is selling anything, unless it is unique there are a big number of vendors, not only selling the same thing, but making the same preparation, maybe even paying the same SEO experts, and the end result will be if hundreds of sellers are doing, more or less, similar things, it is not possible to give all of them a good position, whether it is through PPC or not, no matter how much they are willing to pay. We know that there is always a limitation to what anyone of them can pay and it depends on various factors. It is the same with search results, because it is not possible to cram 100 businesses into the first page, and the last one among the 100 ads will have to be on the tenth page, far removed from where anyone will want to visit.

So, what could we conclude from these? Is it impossible to do business online? It is not, but those who are running brick-and-mortar have the advantage of serving a given locality, which could be enough for their business. Even there if their number is high, naturally some of them have to go, because there is not going to be enough business going around for all of them. As a result, some of them could search for locations that are not saturated, and in their lifetime they might have to change locations several times simply because one location could get crowded by those who are giving similar services who could be new entrants or are changing locations.

Nevertheless, the Internet is different, especially because of what is happening, where one search engine is becoming too popular, and that is where everyone comes to do business. They all prefer to go to Google, whereas Yahoo for example is as good as Google if not better, although that is slowly changing. That has nothing to do with the service it offers except the number, which could be driven by myth. Yet, it does not mean Google could not be playing its card better in some cases where for example the AdWords PPC program is much simpler and faster to get started than others. That might be due to the rules, for example, Yahoo and the other search engines where paid advertising is involved have put in place, and Google's offer is simple and straightforward, even if Yahoo's is very similar. Yet, there are few things like what Yahoo has what it calls paid inclusion, where those who do not pay will lose out from the cream of the crop. In PPC advertising, Yahoo had made it a rule that every application needs revision and it might take a few days, but Google had made the process almost immediate. A few things like these might make a big difference.

Yet, people are made to believe that unless they do business on Google, or if buyers and searcher do not visit Google, they might miss out a lot, but those who know what is happening, more or less, know they are the same except that it is the hype-driven searchers that are flocking to Google. If we come to think of it, there is not a single entity that would not put their material on Yahoo if they put it on Google, maybe with a very few exceptions. If we take the robots both are using independently, they are at par, which means they go out regularly and index sites as long as they are somewhere on cyberspace. There are even reports that stated that as far as indexing and visiting already indexed sites are concerned for some reason Yahoo leads the way with a huge margin. When it comes to indexing Yahoo gives priority to its paid inclusion, but it indexes new sites at the same rate as Google, with even fewer requirements, and the treatment sites get at Yahoo is much better, and this is a fact that can be tried.

The problem might be using two search engines for PPC marketing might not make sense and everyone has zeroed in on Google to make it the place to be. The key here is making a business available at the two sites might give a relief to the bottleneck and the congestion created at Google. From past experience there might be buyers who are bargain-hunting and after visiting a site say, for example, at Google and costing the advertiser the PPC rate, they could go and encounter the same site at Yahoo and might make him incur another PPC rate. This outlook could be defied as long as the material is the same and when people see the same advertising at Yahoo it would definitely ring a bell and they will skip it, because they will be spending time for nothing. Alternatively, it is not a bad idea simply to take a chance on one search engine, because there are still a big number of visitors that prefer Yahoo and why not do business with them.

Since many people are choosing to do business with Google there is a bottleneck, not for the buyers mind you, because no matter what, the buyers will find what they are looking for, yet they might be shortchanged and sites they are encountering might not be the ones that are offering the best value. Search engines do not compare values, and they have no means of telling which site is doing good business from the buyers' perspective, because that is how the robots are programmed. They do not compare prices or other niches each site is offering to the consumers, and if they do, the game would have been different. Their job is if there is anyone who can pay the highest bid among those who are paying for advertising they will get the top spot. Those who could be doing presumably the job better by offering better value for the consumers are left out because they could not bid out of their senses, and there is not much anyone could do about it. That is why the Internet is still an untamed jungle.

Therefore, it is possible that those who could have been offering the best deal for the consumer could have been locked out and to find them buyers might have to go up to the tenth or even more results to compare price, and it is doubtful if they do it. However, the good thing is the paid ad is not yet crowded as the other search results are, which means visiting the ten or so advertisers will not be a problem. But there is one catch, because those ads displayed are not all the ads that should be displayed for the keywords, and as we know it those ads we see displayed are those that are paying the highest bids whatever their amount is, and those that are not bidding high enough will get so many impressions only, which will be less than those that are willing to pay higher bid for the same keywords.

However, not everyone uses the same keywords and it is very difficult to advise on what kind of keywords to use. Yet, each search engine displays for those who want to see what kind keywords are used often, the number of their frequency accompanying them, as well how much money bidders had been willing to pay for them. In other words, how much click through rate each keyword commands. Conventional wisdom has it that using those exact keywords that are displayed there will put everyone on the same wagon, and it is only those who will bid high for those keywords that will pop up when search is conducted. Using a little bit altered keywords might bring those using them out of the same pack and give them some uniqueness and doing that might even do something good for their pocket.

It could also go either ways, because they might miss out on the "hot keywords" and the final decision-makers are those who are choosing keywords, and they always have to experiment on what will work better for them. Mixing the "hot keywords" with less used keywords might create opportunity for some or sticking it out with the less used words might give some, the winning combination. However, what most people recommend is not to go for those single keywords even if we have tried to show that outlook might not be correct for the most part, where there might not be many one word "hot keywords".

If someone uses the keyword "car", for example, things related to cars are huge. There are dealers, there are repair shops, there are those who sell parts, those who rent them, those who park them, those who store them, and the list could go on. If someone wants to buy a car and the car bought is going to be a used one, saying so will make a heck of a difference, because those who are selling used cars will pop up at the top making things easier for the searcher. Therefore, for the most part, with some exceptions, one-word keywords might not be effective. Yet, what is recommended is a phrase of two or three words or even more words that will precisely express what is needed, then the results could be as close as possible to what is needed, and at least the first ten list might have what is required.

How to Beat the Vagaries

The whole idea of the undertaking is to drive traffic to a web site so that it is possible to conduct some kind of business. The traffic for the most part could be a qualified traffic, because such particular traffic encountered the site, more or less, searching for what the site is offering and the chance of closing a deal is much higher. Other than that, there is no guarantee that every click through would mean business, but the majority of it could be so. But when we see what is happening in the PPC bidding, doing business that way could be expensive for some, because of the high bidding rate there are ads that do not show often to bring in the required volume of business. When this happens there are more choices out there and one of them is to increase the bidding rate with the hope that enough traffic could find its way to the site or find other ways of augmenting the traffic.

Even some businesses might do just fine amid all the bidding war, simply because what they are doing could be unique or there are not many people doing what they are doing, and the rest should look for alternatives. One of them like we said it is a well generically kept site so that whenever someone uses their keywords the site will pop up, not only in the paid ad section, but among the search results holding a good position, like for example the first two or three pages of the search result so that what could be falling behind with paid ad marketing could be supported by the generic marketing. We have touched on how SEO companies can make a difference even if they are not a sure thing either and it had been demonstrated why they could fall short.

One good statistics figure that can tell us what is happening between SEO and paid advertising is 83 percent of businesses use PPC while only 11 percent of advertisers use generic advertising and those who could be mixing both might fall in the 11 percent range. This shows that most businesses that already have put aside a marketing budget would prefer to go out there and start doing business immediately, because why wait so long and bother with SEO techniques to work. Some SEO experts claimed that at times what they are preaching sounds like a voodoo magic rather than a practical one, because it could work or not. Yet its main attraction is it could do some good for those who are trying the water with a shoestring budget.

The other lucrative way of reaching unqualified traffic is email campaign even if we know that most of it could be labeled as junk mail. Nevertheless, even sales people who are pounding the pavements on a daily basis will have so many doors slammed on their face before they get a few prospects, which means what is taking place in email marketing is a common scenario in the world of cold-calling. At times, the price could also be affordable. There is an advertising that usually arrives through email, and it is a junk mail for the most part, since they sent it out through automated process. What it advertises is email marketing. It says they will send email marketing to 150,000 addresses and the ad starts only at $9. That is a difficult offer to refuse if someone had been contemplating to try email marketing campaign. While visiting the site it is possible to find out that the company promises to send out 10,000 emails on behalf of the customers for only $9 and to send 150,000 email it costs close to $92.

Now, if we do the math and if only 10 percent of the 150,000 responds for the ad and only seven percent buys, what we are talking about is close to 1050 closed sales and this kind of sales figure could be realized within the same week the email had been sent out. This might not be such a bad result at all depending on what one is selling. And there are some that will charge more but they promise to send millions of emails on behalf of their customers, and no matter how many they send out, even if most of them are rejected, there could be a good amount of sales closed. That is what those who are against such method of advertising are moaning about, because no matter how many of the email is filtered and labeled as junk, these people still get away by making good money, which makes it a reasonably good business.

Recently Yahoo and AOL have announced to introduce a plan that will charge each email from .004 up to .01 and they guarantee that those emails will go through the filtering without being labeled as junk. It is possible, in spite of the fact that the recipients will have to agree in advance to receive the emails that most of the businesses that are engaged in email marketing would take this route. It, of course, adds more expense on their existing cost, but they can see many people find these emails in their inbox instead of in their junk email, because naturally, since the inbox is mostly reserved for email that is not automatically generated, their chance of being read is high, and that is what these marketers are exactly looking for. Not all automated email might be junk. They will be in to make a lot of money, because we know that there are people with a lot of money that do not know how to use it effectively and these marketers are going to tell them that there is something they can offer them and more and more people will start doing business using this method.

This means the rate of $92 to reach 150,000 prospects is very reasonably priced as long as they keep their word, which could be found out from those who had done business with the company, and certainly there could be a blog talking about email marketers. That is where people could find out about these kinds of businesses.

Talking about blogs, they are one great source of traffic like it had been touched on, because the webmaster could put different material about what the site is doing and chances are if it is done on a regular basis the blog itself could pop up when search is made, because the webmaster will have to make sure to use those particular keywords that are being used whether for PPC advertising or for the generic one. This option is going to be a third means of advertising that is floating in cyberspace to pop up every now and then when the keywords are used. Do not rule out the chance that it could outdo the other two, because most search engines, in addition to including blogs in their search results, they have put a means in place to search only for blogs.

As a result, typing on those search engines that are only showing blogs in their search results "email marketing companies", sites that specialize in email marketing will pop up and it is no wonder if most of them have their own blogs. On the other hand, if that is not the case, somehow blogs that could be talking about email marketing companies are the ones that will pop up in the search results. As a result, what we are looking at here is one web site that it is doing the same thing could have four outlets, at least up to this point and that is a good amount of exposure where the cost could be put at a minimal. The PPC with $1 daily budget and .01 click rate could be popping up for the keywords chosen, and if the choosing had been made carefully, there is a chance of doing business there, and that could be tweaked according to the results that is the sales volume. If it is non-existent, it is always possible to add both the daily maximum and the per-click-through rate. This can be monitored either by the amount of money made or it is possible to put one of those free counters on a site to see how many visitors it has.

The generic marketing could be undertaken by the webmaster and what the SEO experts do had been touched on slightly, even if they might have more techniques that are out in the open. We do not have to forget the black hats and at the time of this writing the site of BMW that was selling used cars was in the news because it was banned by Google for using black hat tactics. What they did was to give it a rank of zero so that it will not show up in the search results simply because it was caught while using black hat technique to get the top spot. Yet the general SEO techniques like the meta tags that could easily be generated by sites such as scrubtheweb.com for free are essential and at the reach of everyone. The rest have to do like it was mentioned to use highlighting for some of the key words or repeating them several times, not more than three times though, in the body and at the end of the page and the keywords will make the site avail what the search engines are looking for. The webmaster could do all this, which means there is no expense related to it.

On top of this, by simply starting a blog, two advantages could be availed with the search engines alone that is without mentioning what the blog could accomplish after it is found with would be prospects. The blog carrying, more or less, similar messages in a blog format are going to pop up everywhere when those keywords are used. That is unmatched double advantage. When we take into consideration what the blog will give us, a one-on-one opportunity with prospects to exchange ideas and more that will definitely outdo traditional sales people that will have to pound the pavements on a daily basis. Even to make things more a web site can have a chat or a forum with not cost at all, although having a chat going might require someone there all the time. If the webmaster have the time it will save a lot of money.

Even if the short cut is PPC advertising, it does not come cheap for most. Yet, still the money businesses pay for PPC advertising when compared to radio, TV, or newspaper ad could be reasonable. Classified ads still might be cheaper, because with the arrangement we discussed PPC could cost an advertiser $60, $90 or $150 a month after doing a lot of advertising where a classified ad, let alone the others, just for a week might cost more than $60 and it is difficult to say which one is more effective. Yet, recently, both search engine companies Google and Yahoo have started to open venues for their advertisers by working with the print and radio media where it is expected the cost will be low. However, still in order to do a very effective business doing offline advertising also is recommended, and as long as long as prospects know the URL, they might want to pay the site a visit. To come back to our point here, as we know it, the best advantage of the Internet is diehard businesses could try to do business without spending any money for advertising, and get away with it. And when they start earning income they could have enough budget to look say for example the PPC way, but the PPC is not a must requirement for startups, but when combined with all the available channels it could do wonders. Or those who can afford to cover the expense might not have to waste their time with the other means.

Nevertheless, they could miss out, because there are still many other sources from what we mentioned above that are a source of traffic. Reciprocal links that are part of the SEO strategy have some use in generating traffic, but because if going the generic way alone, search engines do penalize if the reciprocal links do not have relevance with what the site is doing and this kind of fallout hamstrings a fortified effort of creating a big number of reciprocal links. Reciprocal links could also be bought and a site could have thousands of links that do not have relevance to what it is doing could be made to point at it. What that means is traffic could find its way to the site through such links and it could be in a sizeable amount. In addition, the webmaster can scour for sites that are looking for reciprocal links and doing it on the site is possible or sometimes it requires sending out emails.

The issue of building reciprocal links might have not been touched on thoroughly, but since it is a source of traffic that is, without mentioning that some of the search engines have made it a requirement and it is through such links they can judge the popularity of sites, it is needless to say they are very important. But one key issues here is there is going to be a choice to be made either to meet the search engines' requirements where all reciprocal links have to have relevance or to go out and use them as a source of traffic. Because one of the oxymoron here is if a site sells books, it is not only those that are doing things related to writing who only buy books. In fact, it is the general public that could be visiting any site. An online shoes store, an online deli, an online garage, an online car dealer, an online car part seller, an online site of a home-hardware store, and the list goes on. Anyone who is visiting these sites might also be interested to buy books that a particular site is selling. As a result, if they stumble upon the site chances are they want to see what is offered and the chance of their buying is also there, because if they are not interested they would not visit. And if the captivating design to build confidence and the first impression, the copy, and the product are there, there could be a closed deal right there.

Even if it is difficult to show search engines these particulars, there has to be a way to circumvent them, because it is only Google that has this kind of strict requirement and they might know it that they are making a mistake. Yet, lately the importance of reciprocal links have become less and most SEOs are aware of it. Nevertheless, since it is not dropped completely it could penalize a site which otherwise could get a good position in the search result.

It might work if there is another site that is solely soliciting for such links and it does not necessarily have to have an exact similar site with the other one the webmaster is using, to get a good rank with Google or the other search engines, because there is also what is called content duplication that we have not mentioned that will result in penalizing a site. Most probably we might have touched on this when we talked about putting borrowed content that are available for free on a web site, because if they are used in other places and if the robots find out they penalize the site. The same goes with similar sites, but making sites different even if they are using the same domain with a different extension is not difficult, and this one might not have to be a hot looking site, just a working site others will link to, and there will be a blog link that will lead to the site that is doing the main business. And here it is possible to use a different service since there are a good number of them that provide a free space.

The result will be visitors that encounter the links on these reciprocal links could find their way to the site and the search engines might not know whether the site is directly related to the other site, they might even consider it as another incoming link. It has to be like this because a huge traffic could be generated through this and the way many sites are avoiding the penalty is they either run an index site or if they are using PPC effectively that is if they can afford it they do not have to play ball with search engines to give them good position on their search results. What this tells us is whether we can afford the PPC advertising within a given budget parameter or we have decided to go through the generic way for a while or permanently if we want to do business, we have to direct enough traffic to the web site, and this is among the few ways of accomplishing that.

Exploring more Possibilities

In order to visit already indexed sites search engines require a good amount of quality original content that will be updated regularly to be in place and that will give them a good reason to come out and visit such sites, whenever new content is being added. Even if the content duplication issue could hang in the air, which means the robot could find out about it if it is in a form of articles it could be sent out to ezines that have a big number of networks that will post this content on their sites. And the originator of the content can promote what it is doing in the box that will always be provided at the bottom of the article and it is possible to include a link through which traffic can find its way to a selling site. Here, the best strategy is not to send the same articles used on the site to the ezines to avoid a bug in an otherwise well performance of the site at the search results. What this means is writing two different articles, even if the topic is the same could go a long way and serve the desired purpose. But if the webmaster is using only paid advertising like PPC it does not make much difference, because a good rank in the search results is not as important as a good rank in the advertised search results.

Even if it is evident that it definitely requires more work if the work is done correctly this is also another source of a huge traffic and the content producer could become as creative as possible, whether with the theme or the articles that are promoting what the site is doing or something relevant or a subject dealing close to what the originator is doing. In reality that is not a strict requirement, because as long as there is a good message in the content, out of curiosity, visitors can flock to the site, and if a good copy is there it is possible to close deals by converting them into buying prospects.

Placing this kind of content on blogs is possible too and the possibility of its starting a discussion is there. The interaction could raise more interest to know what the moderator is doing and visitors could flock to the site, again if there is a good copy it could convert them into prospects. For the most part, visitors like to bookmark a blog so that they could come back and visit it when they have time and these kinds of visitors if not immediately, as long as they know what goes on, they could become future prospects. As a result, what this reveals is the success rate depends for the most part on the amount of effort exerted by the webmaster, and at times the best selling method like PPC alone might not do the job even if the willingness and capability to foot the bidding bill is there.

Big businesses, on top of their PPC campaign, in most cases conduct regular news release that could open a Pandora box, where the media could get interested on what is going on. Because if you read the media regularly, all those well researched articles about what a business is doing are the outcome of press release. The company will send out the press release to various publications and some of them will decide to write about it, because they have to present interesting topics to their audience while at the same time the businesses will get the exposure they seek badly to do business. It is possible to conduct interviews, through either email, telephone, tele-conferencing, or TV appearance that would lead to a good number of possibilities. All along, the company could work on the brand awareness aspect of the business and if anyone from the audience wants to get a better scoop about the company at their own pace they might want to visit the web site that is if they are not yet decided buyers. There the very effective copy will wait for them with the information they need and the possibility of their being converted is there.

The issue here is if someone has an interview on TV or a radio the exposure is huge. The same goes if interviewed by some of the popular publications that have a huge audience. Anyone who follows the URL provided could definitely become a good prospect, because for the most part, people could find all the information they need from the interview, but if that necessitates the visiting of the site, the visitor has passed that 50 percent nodal point to become a buying prospect.

Here also some cost could be realized because there are not many agencies that will do the press release for free, although the webmaster can do it, and all it takes is to prepare a good press release, where there are abundant guides how to write one, then send them out to the known media powerhouses. It is the editors that will decide if the content is worthy of mentioning and since they need good material, as long they know it will not make them lose face, they will assign a staff writer to do more research and investigation, and if it gets the final approval it will be up there in front of everyone. The good thing is even if nothing materializes, just making them do the decision that is the editors or those who are in charge of what has to be aired or published might create some stir that might have a totally new twist in the future.

Even bringing what a site is doing to the attention of a few people is enough, because word-of-mouth itself might give it some boost, but the webmasters should go for maximum exposure and should try repeatedly before they give up, because that is how things work with these media outlets. They are always overwhelmed with material and they will find it difficult to decide which one should get the go ahead, and one way of making them do such a decision is to remind them again and again.

The newsletter also could do wonders even if it is not an easy task to undertake and it might require someone to prepare it, and that might means another expense. If that is not a problem because the business is big and can handle the expense or there could be in-house staff to do it without incurring more expense that is even better. In the case of a small business, the strapped webmaster might have the time to write some ten or more articles on a monthly basis and circulate them. Those who want to put content on an ongoing basis on their web site could use some of it in the newsletter too, because visitors do not mind if they encounter the same material, since they would not visit the site to read the material if they have found their way through the newsletter.

They will be there to know more about the business or what the offer is, and the next natural step is they will become customers. Still the content duplication issue should be kept in mind because it could hamstring the well performance of the web site in the search results, provided that it is on generic SEO that the site is trying to be found on search results. To avoid that, whenever there is a shortage of material, from what is happening in the literary market there are articles that could be bought for $5 or even less and one easy source is Constant Content, for example and for sure there are more. Using these kinds of material on the newsletter might be better at times because the newsletter does not necessarily have to have a direct relation with what the web site that it promotes is doing, although staying around to the core of what the business doing is advised.

While having a newsletter circulating the subscribers are opt-ins, which means their email address can be used to send them sales pitches, even if what they do is receive the newsletter and nothing else. These kind of emails are useful like it was mentioned earlier, because there is no fear that they will retaliate, and if they do not want the sales pitches they have to be given the opting-out clause. However, if they choose to receive the pitches, let them take there time to become prospects and the newsletter would accomplish the job.

Among many things, the newsletter could be used as a medium to teach the subscribers about what the business is doing on an ongoing basis, and it is always possible that the need to do business with the site might be triggered at one point, and if that is not going to be the case, the newsletter is a good tool to build brand awareness. The subscribers, after receiving the newsletter for some time, they will know most of the things they have to know about the particular brand, and if they want more they can visit the web site. If they still need more they can contact the business. So it does not make sense to miss out from this kind of lucrative means of exposing the business to would be prospects. Yet, doing business using most of the methods mentioned here is different from opening a shop somewhere, whether it is online or offline and wait until business comes in.

Amazingly enough that could happen in case of a brick-and-mortar business because it is the location that would do that and for the most part the cost of doing such a brisk business because of a location is included in the rent paid. At times, it could cost an arm and a leg, but making a profit is there too, otherwise the business has to go under.

What about an affiliate program? There is nothing special about it except that it is an invitation to those who will be interested to promote what a business is doing and for doing so, the affiliates will get a certain portion of the sales closed in a form of a commission. This is not a new arrangement, because sales had been around from time immemorial and that was how the traditional salesmen were doing it. No one asks independent salesmen how they are doing what they are doing. Do you they visit their prospects in person? Do they make a house-to-house call? Do they do it business-to-business? Alternatively, do they distribute brochures on behalf of their customers? Do they call their prospects over the telephone? Do they run a call center that is equipped with paid telemarketers?

What they simply look at is how many buyers they are sending to them and they pay them the agreed upon commission whenever a sale is closed through them. The same goes with affiliates except that for the most part they are doing it online. They can promote the product offline and as long as the prospect does the click through their URL that they will provide when the sales is closed the commission is theirs, because the vendors know through which agreed upon link the buyers came through.

There is a good amount of trust involved here because the affiliates cannot know exactly how many of the clicks that went through their link have made payments for the most part. They can tell how many visitors clicked through their ads. They can also put a polite request to the visitors to send them email if they buy the product by going through their link and most people might be willing. For the most part there is no way of knowing how many people that clicked through the provided ad closed a sale.

Therefore, if a webmaster is using all of the above mentioned strategies it means the webmaster is really running the whole gamut and running a business effectively means just that. Nevertheless, everything depends on the budget because the Internet is a place that attracts a bizarre kind of business people who are full of ideas, but they lack the resources. Stories like "I started out with a telephone and a PC or a laptop and I have already made million dollars sales" abound. Of course, once at this particular juncture webmasters could even do more to make their effort more effective because they have the resources and the probability is they must have used one or more of the routes we are talking about here. But here we are talking with startups for the most part, or those who had been around and are on the verge of throwing the towel because they are not doing the kind of business they went out to do. Or some might be familiar with most of what had been touched on but somehow trying to make it work for them did not materialize in their case, because there could be some bolts and nuts that are missing or they are using them the wrong way.

So to come back to what we are saying here, how about if the webmasters did not want to deal with affiliates, because they thought that it is not cost-effective even if once a web site is made to accept links from various affiliates whose number is high the rest could be automated. Then there should be a tool that will tally all the needed information as to where the sales originated from, and credit the account of the affiliates for future payments, because they are not required to make payment immediate and the job is almost complete.

Nevertheless, how about if such webmasters did not know that there are programs that are very much affordable that will help them to establish themselves into that field. Implementing such a program would mean to avail their business to a huge source of what they need badly, which is traffic. If you ask brick-and-mortar vendors what they need most, you should expect the answer to be customers. The same goes with online vendors, what they need most is qualified traffic and it is after that that they will have what is required to do a genuine business.

What needs highlighting here is every single stage of marketing might have its own independent payoff, but if mixing what are all out there is possible, augmenting the sales volume is there. In fact, except that at a given point the markets could get saturated and if so there is so much every vendor can sell, the sky is the limit. There is no business that says we have got enough and we do not need more than this. There is no business that says we have reached our ultimate goal and taking what we are doing farther is not in our interest. Let us look at companies like Google, Yahoo, or Microsoft as example, because even if they are making a lot of money already, they are always coming up with more products that are needless to mention here. If they do not aspire so they might not be able to do what they are doing. Google would not mind to take the desktop control Microsoft is enjoying and in order to avoid that Microsoft is working hard to take the search control out of Google's hand so that it will not be a threat. This kind of competition is everywhere and businesses that do not innovate will perish and that is just a given natural law.

For startups, it could be like aspiring to become a huge fish, which might sound like unnatural, but somehow in the world of business that possibility is there and in fact that is the way to go. Google started out from a garage, so did Microsoft and look where they are today. Yet, what needs realizing here is businesses are always wracking their brain to come up with that wining unique formula, let alone innovating, and implementing what had already been in use.

So, what we are trying to do is if a business is thriving it still could thrive more and the means of attaining that goal might be around and it might be a matter of not spotting it. If a business is having it bad, it might be because there are things it is not doing right. If startups got everything right at the beginning they will save a lot of time and hassle, because the rest will be monitoring and tweaking it here and there. Especially an online business is like a living organism that needs something external for subsistence, maybe for different reasons, or the reasons might be the same. In the case of organisms, there are hosts of things that will need replenishing, because somehow they will get used up. Why, because mostly organisms use energy to survive no matter what their size is. If they do not exert energy, the probability is they are hibernating and they could get away with small amount of energy, which on itself depends on external things.

Even the lowest amount of task in the body needs some energy and we can take as example breathing. If there is not enough breathing no matter how a passive process it might look and if there is not enough energy to suck in air and breathe it out, what will follow is death, because the body system, especially the brain does not work without oxygen that it should get through the blood.

Business is also the same because there are competitors that will suck the available business leaving the others without business. Then how are the others going to carry on? There are bills to pay and falling behind for one month is enough to lose any of the services that require payments. The same goes with the service provider. A telephone company for example if it does not have customers it will have to relinquish its existing customers to a competitor that is still able to do business and go under, which means die like the organisms because the body or the brain was not getting enough oxygen to continue to do what it is suppose to do. So what do living organisms do? No matter what their size is they will have to find the elements that will give them that energy and that is why there is war in the world if we come to think of it, or there used to be war in the world. It was a matter of survival and those who do not have enough should take it from those who have it in abundance, and sometimes it does not matter whether they have it in abundance or not. If someone starves a well-groomed pet dog, do you think it will die putting its head between its paws? It could start by eating the smaller pet, the cat, if it is around for the first night. The next night unless it is fed or destroyed there is a very dangerous problem on hand.

But before reaching that the well-groomed pet's instinct might tell it to go out and get food and there is no better place than hitting the garbage bins in the surrounding area, because they have food in them. How about if it is living in a very remote area? It could be good by to domestication and it will become a hunter and will go after the smaller creatures, then the bigger ones might not be safe either.

Businesses also have to try every available means to carry on with what they are doing profitably. As it was mentioned earlier there is no limit to their success rate, because if a business shows a good success rate it should expand into something more lucrative. Why, because it could be in a position or it will have to do what it is doing better, since there will definitely be competitors that are trying to overtake it, devour on it like wild animal do on their preys. When it goes bankrupt and liquidated, the first ones at the door to buy what it is forced to sell are those that are doing similar things, because they have good use for almost everything it has under its position, as they are doing the same thing, or they could be middlemen that could pass it to those that are in a similar business with the bankrupt business.

The same thing happens in the big waters. Bigger fish is living on smaller fish and there is nothing that changes that. Men cannot change that even if they feed themselves continuously on the bigger fish. Men also cannot change competition in a market economy because it is part of doing business better and only those who do things better survive at the end of the day, which is good for the consumers because they are served by those who offer the best, and it is the consumers who make the final judgement by parting with their hard earned money. One known means of surviving method is just trying everything available, yet the way of implementing them differs according to the resources and the stage the business is at.

Even if PPC advertising is lucrative if someone is not realizing any advancement using the system what is required might be to stand back and consider trying the generic route, because it is better than quitting. The webmaster himself can do it by saving himself/herself all the involved expense and at one point going back to PPC might become attractive and profitable because the requirements could be met better due to the preparation made using a less intense method of marketing. As a result when startups try the water using cyberspace they have an unprecedented advantage to succeed with whatever they are doing because people are buying a lot on the Internet. If not replacing the offline businesses, stand-alone businesses with the right kind of product and preparation could make profit on the Internet.

Up to this point, we have touched on the general picture of what it means if someone is contemplating to start a business on the Internet or if someone is trying to resuscitate a business that had gone numb. In the following section we will focus on strategies that are deemed to show result if they are experimented with, because we have said online business is like a living organism and it is very much different from brick-and-mortar that only needs a good location. Online there is no static location as such, but there is a dynamic location that shifts all the time.

There is no such a thing as saying that I have rented this particular location and I am entitled to it legally as long as I continue paying for it. On the Internet the domain name or the URL might belong to the owner that paid for it, but the location of business being the search results, there is not guarantee a site that had been first on a given search result for a given keyword will stay first always. Someone else will take that spot within the hour and all the site can do is work furiously to attain that spot and there is no legal system that will guarantee that the spot will be his/hers even if he/she pays any amount, because someone paying only .01 more can take that spot.

But there is a dynamic system that "could" guarantee that spot for the webmaster and that is what we are working at here. To make the webmaster familiar with the dynamic system so that he/she will know how to use it to get the best position in the search results that being the dynamic location where anyone doing business online can open shop. This is applicable for any businesses small or big that you can name. Businesses can get the top spot because they are paying the top bid, which could go up and down, even then there is not guarantee they will keep it constantly, because it had happened many times.

A must Have Tools to Promote a Business Online

We have been generalizing all along just to make sense by what we mean doing business online, because we know that the Internet is a fairly new medium, and it is gradually that it evolved into a marketplace where any kind of business could be conducted. The key concern while doing business is whether it is worth the time and money invested into it or not, because if there is no return, all the efforts will not only go down the drain, but it had been a waste of time and resources. That is what we are trying to prevent here, because it had been proven that it is very possible to do a profitable business on the Internet, but in order to do that there are certain things that have to be done. Moreover, the key here is marketing, and when we say marketing we are looking at a fairly vast subject matter. What needs to be accomplished is giving a sound service that could either be selling products or selling services where anyone should be able to do a profitable business. What is good about the Internet is very effective tools had been developed to enable any business to do a profitable business. Consequently, making oneself familiar with these tools is paramount to anything and should come prior to the final strategy.

Pay Per Click Advertising

This tool is what is doing wonders out there and it was Overture that introduced it before Yahoo bought the company. However, it was Google that found out its potential and along the way, it made billions of dollars through it. Its share was at $80 at the time of its IPO a few years ago and recently it was selling around $500 and close to 99 percent of its source of income originates from PPC advertising even it is trying to diversify furiously. What we have got here is like it was mentioned earlier, an advertising system that anyone can start with a $5 dollar activation fee and a maximum daily balance of $1 and a PPC rate .01 and it does not get any cheaper than this, because there is no any advertising method that is as cheap as this one.

As anyone could find out from the AdWords site on Google's homepage, it takes only a few minutes to get started, one of the major differences with Yahoo's Overture, which is, more or less, the same except that to start advertising with Overture it will take several days until someone approves the process, which means there might be a possibility of being declined. Someone has to pore into what the applicants want to do maybe to prevent someone from being unethical! The Google team does the same too, but until they approve or disapprove an applicant the ad will go live and after that the similarities kicks in. Yet, it suffices to say that Overture is not hands-off like AdWords whose requirements are to have an account in a form of a credit or a debit card from where they will deduct the cost of getting started. Wiring money to both of them is also possible, but they will have to wait until they receive the wire to activate the account.

There are two kinds of payment arrangements, and one of them is Post Payment, where all expense incurred in a month will be deducted at the end of the month. The other arrangement is depositing a certain amount of money and when that fund runs out, either Google will debit the accounts for more or the advertiser could replenish the fund.

Once the decision is made to use their advertising program the second key aspect to do is to work on the text of the ad that would be displayed and here like we mentioned it earlier, it is important to be concise about what the business is doing, because there is not much room to beat around the bush. The system allows 25 charters in the title and there are two lines with 35 charters in each of them and this seems to be much, but it is not and using it wisely is required. In PPC advertising keywords are chosen too and they are much more effective than organic advertising, because the search is conducted by using them, by charging the rate earmarked to each keyword.

Each keyword chosen has a rate attached to it and if it is higher than what is agreed upon to pay as a per click rate, the advertiser has to agree to pay the going rate in order to activate them and the site is found according to the keywords chosen strictly, there are no other ways. Having the main keywords to reflect what the site is doing is very important. Because, putting the keywords in the text does not help at all like it helps in generic search results, because each keyword requires payment in order to include the particular site in the sponsored list.

If an advertiser is willing to pay .01 per click on a certain keyword if that keyword is found to cost more, in order to use that keyword, to activate it, and to start using it that amount should be paid, and for the most part it depends on what the webmaster is doing. There could be keywords that will cost .10 or .25 even more depending on how often they are in use and how much others had been willing to pay for them. But, all in all, the rate is livable for the most part, but the key to beat in this section is to choose various keywords directly related to what is being done, as many as possible, so that some of them will be more affordable than the others. Even here, using phrases than one-word keywords will bring the cost down, this means it is not that intimidating or unaffordable.

If there is any other expense there is what is called impression and it is the number of times the ad was shown on various web sites that are in Google's network and when that number reaches 1000 the webmaster will pay .25, which is miniscule by any standard when compared with what is done and there is no other cost unless someone clicks through the ad. Here brand promotion is possible without paying much because it is possible that the visitors can see the ad even if they do not click through it, and the more they see it, the chance of their becoming familiar with it is there. To get more impression it is possible to pay more money.

What is great about PPC is it is the advertiser's money that do the talking and it does not matter if the web site meets the requirements the search engines have put in place, and for most businesses it is the fastest way to start an online business. If there is a catch, it is when the number of people doing similar things goes through the roof. When that is the case, in order to sell, webmasters have to spend too, and their home-take profit will be what they make on the difference, which could be low or high. It could become expensive and that is when people will have to be bearish with the expense, yet seeing others bidding more and walking away with their business could understandably be grilling. But the good thing about it is among those who are doing similar businesses if one business can get away making money by spending a lot on advertising and if they happen to carry the same product the others should also do the same, but because there are more means to do business or to outdo each other, the nature of the business will get complicated.

If those who are paying a lot for advertising want to pass the cost to the consumer, when the consumer starts shopping around there is going to be losing business to those who are not charging high. On the other hand, there is no such a thing as selling for a loss, because without a profit no one will do business. This means there is a natural check and balance in place, but some smart businesses could get around it by introducing different methods of doing businesses, and the trick they use could be anything. Some of their introductions might go unnoticed because people have so much time and patience to shop around and they do not come into the marketplace with a catalogue telling them what the price of each good and service is. What happens is if they believe a given product or service has a fair price and have the value they are looking for they would pay for it.

Therefore, what takes place at the marketplace is complex and if every sales is analyzed it might or might not be possible to see a pattern why it should be like it is, but for the most part there is a certain amount of business to be done on cyberspace. The problem is if it is only those that can afford to pay the going bid that are popping up, the rest could suffer a lot and that is why biding comes into the picture and could go either ways; it could become expensive and unprofitable or it is affordable but it eats into the profit that is made. That is when people look at other alternatives. However, it seems that as long as they can live with the bidding rate, they might not have to look at other alternatives, and unfortunately, that does not seem to be true always.

Come on in Search Engine Optimization

SEO has become the second important tool because webmasters are looking for a backup to their PPC advertising that will bring up their web site at the time of search when someone uses their keywords. At times, they might not be into what they are doing for the sole purpose of reaping a benefit immediately, but if they make money they will be happy. This group's intention might not stop here, because they might not want to take the PPC route. The reason they choose the generic route is they are aware of the other available tools that we will touch on as we go along that they believe are cost effective to do business on the Internet. No one can believe this group because we know that there are sites that are popping up at good positions, say the first page or the first three pages, and to be honest people are looking at those web sites when they do search, and those paid ads that pop up around are more or less secondary or supplementary or auxiliary. They mostly are good for those who are shopping. Also lately they could be plagued with those mini sites that are putting endless maize of ads that are difficult to come out of and they are all catering for the AdSense advertising.

Armed with this reality they might know that it is not paying for the PPC ad alone that will bring their site on top of search results where brisk business is done, because savvy searchers look at both results, the main search results, and on the paid ads. What is giving them good position on the search result is good SEO and unless the webmaster is not equipped with the know-how it is going to cost money, but since it is a one-time cost for the most part, it might not be as expensive as PPC. Or the webmaster can do the up-keeping and the monitoring. Whatever the reason, even if it is not much, there is a sizeable demand for SEO and we have said 88 percent prefer PPC, the shortest route to do business immediately, albeit it could be expensive, and the generic route is only favored by the 11 percent, which is better than nothing, but it is time consuming, plagued with uncertainty, and to some extent we mentioned it is viewed like a voodoo technique people have to believe in, just to do the job and it will do it. The other question is 11 percent of what figure, and finding out that could be staggering, yet even the Internet has, more or less, more than one billion participants, and those who are doing business could be in the millions.

Nevertheless, there might be some truth in it because the basic SEO the search engines are relying on to quickly index a site, to give it a good position on the search results is not anything mysterious since it is out there and the search engines themselves talk about it. It could be done when the site is designed, because a good site design is a vital part of an SEO. PPC advertising method does not care about what is happening on a site as long as it falls among those they consider to be binding by the acceptable legal parameter. The site should not engage in any activity deemed illegal, or is not for hate mongering, blasphemy, and the like. When sites meet such requirements all they have to do is just display the ad and let the visitors decide about what they encounter, because they can report a site if they believe what it is doing is out of whack. We know from experience that even if visitors are time-strapped, they should see something fairly good to be convinced that they are doing business with someone they can trust. The design might just tell them that or it might not, because the best designs cost money and all those who can afford to pay might not be doing something deemed decent.

If there is no good copy to tell them why they should buy a product or service, what is involved, what to do when they are not satisfied with the product or service after they paid for it, there might not be anything that will compel them to do business. There should also be a good copy telling them how to use the product, why it is different from similar brands, how much discount they will get, or if there are some add-ons they will get by doing business with the given web site. Otherwise, even if all that is demonstrated seems to weigh better than the rest of the site that they could have seen or could see, why would they want to do business with a given site? The need all these to help them with their decision-making to distinguish the good ones from the bad ones. Sometimes, even if they know what they want to buy, they might want to be educated.

If someone wants to buy an earphone among various models and makes, with their own price range and some advantages they have over the others, the buyer can make an informed decision if a tool to make a good comparison is in place, because the buyer could have come only to buy an earphone without having a special brand in mind. But if the buyer is made to know that there are better headphones that last longer or there are headphones with mikes that could give service and cost the same, such details might be helpful to change the buyer's mind.

While visiting such sites that is what exactly should take place. There should also be comment included by users or product description by those who know more about the particular product. Buyers will definitely walk away from a site that is only selling one earphone, it might not even have a picture of the earphone neither, and all it has is a brand name that sounds strange, let alone to be a household name. This is bad copy, because it is not helping the buyer to make an informed decision.

But if someone is selling Windows NT 4.0/2000 online they might not need even to show any kind of a package, because everyone knows what it is and what it does. What is interesting is there are sites going around strong, selling these kinds of popular software form a word document and as long as there pricing is good they can do good business. But, all the rest should be accompanied with a lot of information if selling them is intended and they should look professional since first impression is always important.

As a result, at least both good web design and a good copy have to go hand-in-hand with whatever the buyers will be seeking. If they are not in place, even if one is using PPC advertising, which is a shortcut to bring a buyer to a site, what does the selling is what is on the site, namely copy. The SEO jargon does not have to be on the web site as such while using PPC except the basic tags, in case the robots encounter the site. Google could index a badly done web site and simply applying for the AdWords campaign will expedite the indexing process with Google. As we all know it unless there is at least a title tag the web site looks funny when it is availed on the search result, but if it is accessed through PPC ad no one will see that and what is required are good design and effective copy.

Which means whether it is to save money or to increase the site's traffic, most of the expenses could be a one-time affair although the organic way is time consuming and at the end might not even be that cheaper than PPC. But there are ways to open even more traffic floodgate, and that is why the generic route is also sought after and is an important integral part in creating an effective tool to take the marketing campaign one notch further.

SEO experts have tried to make the subject too complicated but it is still possible to look at the bare skeleton of what they do for the most part and decide if it deserves all the complication.

<!DOCTYPE html PUBLIC "-//W3C//DTD XHTML 1.0 Transitional//EN" "http://www.seo-oo.org/TR/xhtml1/DTD/xhtml1-transitional.dtd">

<html xmlns="http://www.seo-oo.org/1999/xhtml">
<head>
<meta http-equiv="Content-Type" content="text/html; charset=utf-8" />

<title>SEO Book ON Sale.com</title>
<meta name="Description" content="Search Engine Optimization Book is a SEO blog which provides daily search engine / search engine marketing news. SEO Book keeps up with the latest trends in search engine algorithm changes and provides daily search engine optimization tips. SEO Book offers a search engine optimization ebook for sale."/>
<meta name="Keywords" content="seo book, seo tutorial, seo tutorial book, search engine optimization, search engine optimization tutorial, search engine optimization ebook, search engine optimization ebooks"/>

What is up here is where the SEO work starts and to see what is involved all it takes is to find any web site, click on view, click on source, and it is possible to see what kind of SEO techniques the site has used. We are not concerned about the first part because every web site has a different one depending on what kind of service provider the site is using or who designed the web site if not who did the SEO for the site. Some meta tag generators like scrubtheweb.com will put their name under the tag, but for the most part SEO companies do not do that.

Our interest here starts from where it says <title> and the name of the site used is changed for our purpose here to <title>SEO Book on Sale</title> this tag is key because it tells the search engines what the name of the site is, it is this title that you will see on the search results, and this is the entry point for the robots.

Then comes the "description content" and it might be a little bit too much because if it is more than search engines allow, it will be penalized. What it means in this case is the content that deemed to be extra will be cut off and the remaining portion will be displayed. If there is any casualty because of such action, it is that the message sent out might not be coherent and it has to be made as short as possible. Sites like scrubtheweb.com recommend the title to be made up of 60 characters and the content 150 characters, and any thing more than that could be labeled not search engine friendly and could be truncated.

Other than that there is no harm done because still a good portion of the message will be on display. One key issue to add here is in the "title tag" and "description content", it is highly recommended to put the main keywords sparingly, that is using them in the title and sentences, because when the search queering is done, search engines do not go as far as the keywords, although no one says anything about it, but it helps to know that counting on keywords alone would do the site a big disservice when it comes to organic search results.

For example, if you look at the above example it is possible to find the site for what is on the title, which is "SEO Book on Sale". Also it could be found for "Search Engine Optimization" because it is in the content. But it will not be found for "SEO Tutorial" because anything that has to do with "Tutorial" is shown only in the "keywords" section and there is nothing anyone can do about it, because that is how it works. Therefore, all intended keywords will have to either be in the title or in the content in order to be found with them, one good lesson to remember. Nevertheless, keywords if they are once activated they work great in a PPC campaign.

If any web site has this, its chance of being found is always there, which means webmasters will have to see if this thing is there, exactly like they want it, again with the keywords sparingly dispersed in both the title and the content. If a webmaster is using a site building wizard, the wizard will do it. If it is an SEO expert doing the job, it will definitely be more correct. However, web designers might not do it correctly. If a webmaster uses the free available templates on the Internet for building web sites, they do not have any idea about what the site is doing, which means it would require tweaking.

So, that is the key entry for the search engines' robots and for the most part if they find that is in place, they are out immediately. There are a few things SEOs are talking about including putting some of the keywords around the body of the web site, of course, by putting them in a meta tag and highlighting them helps. Because the robots pick anything that is highlighted. Putting what you put on top of the page at the bottom of the page is also considered good by the robots, but no one tells you why. Yet, as it was mentioned, do not overstuff the keywords, because there is a penalty for it.

This part, however, can be done by the webmaster and there is no need for SEO experts, but they still have advantages because they know which keywords work well thanks for their experience. Most of them recommend wordtracker.com that has a better capability to analyze which keywords will be more suitable for what a web site is doing. There could be others too that are worth checking.

Reciprocal or Incoming Links

This tool used to have a key importance on most search engines, especially in Google because it is through this tool they can gauge how popular a site is. The assumption of this reasoning is if a site has authority in what it is doing, definitely those that are doing, more or less, similar things would like to interact with it, or at times they might not have a choice. A bookseller has to interact with a book distributor or a publisher and would like to direct visitors there to do certain things. If someone wants to sell a book through the store, it will ask visitors to come through the distributor and there will be a link on the site. It might be fashionable to have a link to one or more distributors or publishers. That way if many bookstores have links to the distributor the assumption of the robot is it is popular and Google gives point based on that. To find out more about this particular point, using Google's toolbar is required, and it is possible to download it free from Google's web site. There is a point given from 1-10 and 10 is the highest point, and what it means is the particular site is very popular.

It is not only that any site that has an incoming link from such a site that has a 10 point could end up having its site indexed quickly. Just for your information there are sites that are making money on their popularity and if a webmaster pays $150, for example, the site the webmaster is running could have an incoming link from some popular sites with a 10 point and if it is a new site it will be indexed quickly. If the webmaster does not want to pay the money, because this kind of fee could recur on a monthly basis he or she could discontinue paying once the robots have indexed the site. It will not be deleted from the list of the search engines, but it might affect its ranking in the search result, because if not all, most sites that end up at the top have good points if not exactly ten, and like it was mentioned earlier trying to obtain this point quickly by links could lead to the site being penalized.

What this reveals is reciprocal or incoming links are a way to tell the search engines that the site is an authority in what it is doing. Nevertheless, using a white hat technique will take a while to obtain all these lists to point at a given web site. There are many ways to do it and among the good jobs SEOs accomplish is they can build a good reciprocal link for their customers over time and that could cost money. If the webmaster wants to do it, it will take a lot of time if not money and there are software that can do it with a relative ease and speed. Even if simply pressing a button could send out the email, it would not change the time it will take to get a reply, and because of that, search engines do not consider it a black hat technique.

One good software that can do that is Seoelite and the way it does it is, by simply typing in what the site is doing it will bring up sites that are doing similar things. From there on it is just a matter of picking the site that is on top and enter the URL in the space provided while opening the software. Followed that there are a few things that can be done and one of them is to track what kind of web sites are pointing at the site that got the first spot in the search engine result for the keyword the webmaster is using, and the result is all sites that are pointing at the particular site will show.

There are a few things to read from the result, but our concern here is how to send email to all those pointing at the web site and that is done by simply instructing the software to get the contact information for all the web sites shown, and they could be thousands but that result will show. There are templates to choose from to type in the message and by simply hitting a button, all those sites will get the email. It is not only that the software keeps record of which sites had been sent email and how many times. In addition, it is always important to put the links of the sites that were asked to put link on the webmaster's link page and the software will do it with a click of a button. A monstrous task that will take days and weeks could be done within five minutes and what the software costs is around $26 as the writing of this handbook.

Doing it manually is the same except that scouring each site for their email address is required. Some email services automate the whole process of sending out the emails for a large number of recipients. But all the email address has to be typed and we know it is not easy to find where the contact information is, and it is possible to make a mistake while copying the email address unless paste and copy is used. Building reciprocal links is a very tedious job and if a webmaster can contact 20 web sites a day, it is enough for the most part. Imagine what kind of work is required to contact 1000 web sites. Whereas, through the software it is possible to contact up to 10,000 web sites within the hour.

When one thinks of creating an individual link that is a lot of time wasted right there and that is why some webmasters want to pay SEO companies a few hundred dollars to make their web sites ready for the search, because a minor lack of not having what is required could make the site to be found on the 100th page, and that for sure prevents a business from being profitable. If things go right, what the business generates would cover most of the expense incurred.

Copywriting

This is a crucially important tool to close deals, because it has nothing to do with being too complicated really, it is just that the site has to be able to close a sale, and it does not matter how it is done, yet there are certain procedures to follow. There are sites with sketches only and people buy from them. Why? Whether you believe it or not it is the copy that makes people buy. A good copy with a simply made site can build the confidence of the buyers and there has to be something that will tell the buyers that they are on a safe ground and good hands. They would conclude that this seller knows his or her stuff.

Design is important too, because visitors will have to find their way easily, and those who are selling are advised to keep their site simple, though well done, because even while using the fastest connections, cluttered pages take time to load. Some people say the reason why people choose Google over Yahoo could be the simplicity of the site. Yahoo is also aware of that and it has its simple version that anyone can use if they are in hurry or if they do not want to be distracted by the celebrities photos and news that clutter Yahoo's main page. It is called "Yahoo Search" and it is similar with Google search except that it has news headline on it. Yet Google's site has no detraction, it is quick to download, and it has what is required. The most richest company's web site is most probably still the most simplest site.

So keeping this in mind helps, but sometimes it is difficult because there are so many things that have to be put on a web site to show visitors what the site is into and for the most part it does not work. It could take unnecessarily long time to download, and people might curse under their breath saying it would have been better if they had visited the other site, or they might not come second time. So the best way out is to send them to a simple landing page and the contents could be on other sub pages that have a clear link on the main page.

What is known in SEO lingo the onpage and the offpage optimization, which is basically what we have touched on earlier is already done the site is going to be ready to be indexed quickly and once indexed it could possibly get a good position, and that is where the trick is. Because the keywords used are what make the difference. For example if the site is using AdWords it is not easy to tell which keywords were used often and it is not possible to raise the bid so that being found with those keywords will be better. However, others sites such as Yahoo allow a peek of the keywords competitors are using. Here too there are software that can do the same for the generically made sites and SEO companies have them, which means if the site is using the best keywords the other sites are using, its chance of being found will be high. That information is also available from the source page of web sites and it is possible to find out why those sites are getting the top spots, whereas the particular site is lagging behind. Based on that it is possible to improve a position of a site.

Then what comes next is to find a means to bring a lot of traffic to it, because the generic way is good only for those that can attain good position on the search results. The other ways of driving traffic to a site are recommended even for sites that are using PPC because even if this sort of traffic is not targeted like the PPC one, as long as what it takes is on the site, which includes a well written copy, converting some of the visitors to buyers is possible, but like we touched on it, it is time consuming, yet there are others who can do it for the webmaster. Since it is going to be on an ongoing basis, it could be more resource draining than the other methods. Other than that, it is possible to do some business through it.

Email Marketing

Another useful marketing tool that deserves a scrutiny is email marketing. Most people are talking about "permission allowed" email marketing, and what it means is they are hiding from the spam bug. But the truth of the matter is, as along as the opt-out clause is included it is legal to send someone unsolicited email and if the recipient sends in the opt-out message it will strictly have to be followed through and if not, the entity can report it as a spam, and it could start a nightmare with a service provider. There is always a grace period between the opt-out message and the reporting of the email as spam. When that period is over it is always important to take a measure. The good news here is the automatic process does the job by simply deleting the opt-out email on the first instance and the problem will be if the software does not do it.

Secondly, as we all know it many people do not have time to read email generated automatically because it is recognized by the spam filter, which almost all email services have in place, so there is no worry. What is amazing is marketers are trying to get maybe three to six people out of a 100 to open their email and do business with them, and even that could be profitable if the email is going out in mass.

We have said there are a good number of software that are a bit pricey that will do the job. They can send out automated email, they can keep track, and they do it again and again according to what they are programmed to do. One software to remember is Seoelite, which the vendors are using for various purposes, but from what we touched on it is possible to type a keyword and find millions of sites that have similar things to do with a particular site, pick as many as needed, time being the essence, get their contact information, prepare the campaign using the template offered by the software, and send thousands after thousands of email. As long as the opt-out clause is included it is not a spam, it is cold-calling. However, the software has to have a mechanism to handle the opt-out callers, otherwise it is asking for a huge trouble, especially if it is done repeatedly. Most email marketing software and autoresponders have this capability.

So, it is possible to hire someone or a secretary can do it on her spare time if what is involved is a bigger business of that stature. If that is not the case if a webmaster spends one hour a day and sends out 10,000 emails that is enough campaigning. Therefore, the key is putting one's hand on a good software program and the campaign is as good as canned. The material that could go out could be a sales pitch that is not different from an effective copy, and in marketing, the best way to do it is not to try to generate sales from the first pitch. That is why doing it in a newsletter format is a good way to go, as recipients tolerate a newsletter because it has other things to talk about.

Asking the recipient to subscribe at the spot does not turn off many people, especially if it is packed with information, since people feel uncomfortable for the most part to refuse using free information. This means the email campaign could start out in a newsletter format, yet it will involve more work. But in today's world there are tons of free material to use and if it is not free there are places where well written 200 and 300 word articles could be purchased cheaply or can be written easily. Newsletter is the best way to go to start that long-term relationship with prospects that might show some fruition some time in the future.

That does not mean the traditional sales pitch that involves crafty sales copy will not do the job. Most of them tend to be long, and some of them will have repeated options in the middle of the sales copy where there is a link to the buy section. That is if at any point a recipient wants to buy he or she can do so. Nevertheless, lately they are becoming short and to the point, because not many people have the time.

So the best thing to do is the first paragraph have to tell what is involved. A simple we sell this and that product is enough and it is possible to expound on that. If grabbing the interest of the recipient was successful the recipient will continue perusing, but if no interest about what is advertised is generated it is possible that they hit the delete button. For the most part people are curious to see what others are selling and it depends where and when they open their email. If they open their email at work either they will leave it for a latter time or they can hit delete if it is in the junk mail file and hundreds of them could perish where they cannot even be retrieved once the bin is emptied.

That being the case, the reasons why most recipients choose the delete button is the emails are becoming ridiculous. As an example, an email ad will make an offer, some of them very enticing. Such as a camera, a vacation package, a camcorder, laptop, PC, cell phone, and what not, but the point here is the invited participant will have to go into a maze of activities that does not have an end. That is not all, the recipient will have to start by buying certain cheap products that could cost only a dollar or so. Because to get a sizzling vacation package people will be obliged to spend some money and they will start paying the few dollars most of the things cost, but the fact of the matter is there is no end to it. Now, everyone knows that these ads are originating from upwardly smart people that will not offer a thing but want to sell, and once all those small amount of money are paid it is another hassle to cancel them, so at the end they will get away without offering the participant anything but costing a lot of money. So people are happier to hit the delete button, because they are, once bitten twice shy, and if some decent business tries to use the same gimmick, they will dismiss it by the delete button.

Genuine marketers will have to find a way to distinguish themselves from this onslaught and most are coming with interesting catch phrases. They do not at all try to deceive the buyers. In the long run, as the number of honest businesses rise people will like to do business with them without being duped, and those that are whining because of receiving too much junk mail should not say so since the job is made easy for them, to delete it without even looking at it. What the key here is reputation and integrity so that people would be happy and willing to do business online. Without promoting a product or a service there is no doing business and businesses will have to wait until people want to do business with them, but where is the guarantee that they will be made aware of the existence of a given offer at the end of a process. People used to sell things on outside markets and most were using all available means of advertising to attract buyers, and the suggestion is if you are not interested with the promotion and what is offered, please continue doing what you are here for.

Newsletter

Newsletters are super marketing tools because they offer a means to collect opt-in prospects. It is not only that, a sales copy and a newsletter content are totally two different things, because a sales copy is there to sell whereas newsletter starts with educating about what the business is offering or doing. It is not also a requirement to talk only about what the particular business is doing. It is possible to put so many interesting things into a newsletter, even material from other sources as long as the necessary precaution to inform the readers where the material originates is there. Creating tons of links to various informative sources that give more insight into what the industry is in possible.

The whole idea is to gain the respect of the readers as responsible marketers, whether they are first-time readers or subscribers, and here and there sales pitches could be sprinkled, but for the most part avoiding being too aggressive in the newsletter is advised. Also it is possible to send a sales pitch to ezines, because they do not reject it if it is written the right way, but a newsletter with sales pitches put inside it could be circulated by ezines around their networks and that is a big exposure, and always a link to the site could be put anywhere everyone can see it, the idea being promoting a site or a business, but not selling outright. Also all ezines provide a box at the bottom of the article to put some kind of relevant message. But there is a big difference between the two, because the sales pitch is a onetime thing that will expire after it served its purpose, whereas a newsletter could remain in an archive for a long period of time and people could use it for research, reference, or they can quote from it provided that it is well written and if some kind of authority had been demonstrated.

However, avoiding making people feeling guilty should also be considered because, here is this entity sending out this kind of highly informative newsletter regularly, and he or she is also aggressive on the sales pitch, which would be translated into hounding and hammering the would be opt-in to death if a sales pitch is enclosed consistently, but doing it at one point or another is just natural. It shows the relationship with the customer is as good as being a buying customer, because at one point when there is a need they could become buying customers.

It is advisable to avoid being too aggressive because people will feel uncomfortable for not buying something from the business if they were receiving the material on a regular basis. Doing it systematically would enhance the brand building whether it is a big business or a small one. As we know it, none of the small businesses that are popping up everywhere jump on the band wagon of newsletter writing, because it is demanding, it requires authority on the subject matter, otherwise it could fire back. As a result, for the most part, simply mentioning the existence of the site and at what URL the business is conducted would suffice and if the publication is void of direct sales pitches it might be good, because the existence of the newsletter itself does that. This is one way of seeing it and the other way of seeing it is to use the newsletter for both brand and reputation building and as well as for pitching non-stop to the op-tins, and some of them might open their wallets or purses. Some marketers cover the distance to stir sympathy by using some of the things that make people do good or socially acceptable things, and it is up to the webmaster which route to take.

One way of engaging opt-ins into action is by offering them some kind of value that will make them participate in something such as filling out forms and the like, and this could be done sparingly on an ongoing basis so that they will be comfortable with the idea of doing business with the business when the right time comes. Of course, their participation level will get a boost when they start valuing whatever they are getting through the participation is really attractive and useful for them.

Marketing a Newsletter Using Email Marketing

Email marketing is one means to use to promote a newsletter by emailing it to solicit opt-ins from those that are random recipients. The other method is to start email marketing with a direct sales pitch and when the recipients visit the site they will be asked to become opt-ins for the newsletter, which is a good method of obtaining their email address. If they become opt-ins for the newsletter the relationship is going to be at a much higher level because the webmaster only needs their email address to mail them the newsletter on a regular basis and all the sales pitches could be included in the newsletter.

Like we said it, mailing out a newsletter is not an easy undertaking, yet if an in-house staff cannot do it, there was a suggestion how to solve such a problem. It is possible to hire a freelance writer, it is possible to buy content as they are affordable, it is possible to use free content even we have to worry about the penalty that could come about for content duplication. One thing we did not mention was there are companies that will need to know only what the business is doing and some general direction, and they could take it from there. This means they could provide everything for a fee. They will come up with the right kind of material and most of all they could come up with the list, which would save a lot of hassle, but they could charge a good amount of money for the service and mostly they are good for big business. Those who are starting out with a shoestring budget if they can write the newsletter themselves, they can mix it with the available free content, which could be converted easily by tweaking it here and there to avoid being classified as duplicate material, and after all it is only robots out there to outdo, except that they could be smart and stubborn.

Another tool to use for an email campaigning is to start a short tutorial on anything, it will be great if it is about what the business is doing, and it is very much different than a newsletter because of its short duration. For the most part, tutorials are more powerful than newsletters to captivate visitors, because they teach something new, some knowledge that have to be possessed immediately, and as we know it most of the time they are offered for a fee, but when user find them free they will be glad to give their email address. Of course, the webmaster will take the engagement to the next level, by sending them sales pitches by letting them know it is originating from the source that is offering the free tutorial, and a good lasting relationship could be kindled. It is also possible to include about what the business is doing in the tutorial in a subtle manner so that it will not distract the session.

Viral Marketing

Viral marketing is slowly becoming an effective way of doing business and has similarity with email marketing, but this one is different because anyone who is a recipient of an email marketing, a sales pitch, or a material can pass it to anyone considered worthy of knowing about the subject matter. Since people have a big number of intimate connections, be it family related, workplace, or any affiliation, any marketing effort that touches base with these kinds of sources could get a good boost. Knowing the availability of these kinds of sources in advance, enables taking advantage of their existence that could do a lot to the campaign. A webmaster that is promoting a site or a business could reap a benefit depending on the kind of affiliation that is applicable in each case.

The same is true with networking except that networking could involve a wide variety of sources that have the same interest or affiliation. Yet, it is as good as dealing with opt-ins, because individuals usually join networks agreeing to contact other members, and as usual, they will need the opt-out option included on any communicating material that reaches their end.

The affinity could start from a neighborhood with the kind of sport or fitness club involved to the kind of church the webmaster a member is. All this social activities have a big number of participants that would not get overtly upset if someone tries to do business with them.

Blog

Blog has become phenomenally popular because if it is setup its potential to reach a big number of people is high. Here people could stumble on the blog or they could be led to it through the above mentioned methods we had been touching on. Visiting a web site could enable a visitor to know about the existence of a blog and because blogs are known to be lively and full of participation, people might want to know what takes place, and if there are a good amount of information put in place, promoting a brand or what a site is doing could be accomplished on the fly. Any kind of material could be put on the blog and participants can comment on it or give feedback to those that are posting the material.

If there is a new thing taking place in a company and if a blog is there and running, and many people know about it, there is no need to send press release everywhere, although doing so could also have a lot of advantage. Because, the way blogs work is mostly by interest. For example, those who are interested in SEO subject could flock to blogs that are addressing issues related to SEO. Those whose interest is software do the same, they flock after blogs dealing with software. But if there is something good or interesting going anyone can go and join any blog and promote a totally out of context material and get away with if it is done subtly, because those blogs are places where a big participating audience could be found, and none of them will say that they do not want to hear or read anything else than what they come there for.

Although that is a secondary attempt, webmasters can try it to spread the word about what they are doing. Yet, the winning formula is when a webmaster starts a blog that deals with the involved business. Nowadays, blogs are getting special treatment by search engines and they have their own search engines where those that are looking for blogs can go and type a subject matter. What the search results show is only blogs that are dealing with the queried subject, which means search engines are out indexing blogs by the tons and giving them a special treatment. That started taking place because a big number of blogs are coming into existence on a daily basis.

It is not only that there are aggregators that deal with blogs only using RSS and if someone likes a particular blog it is a matter of adding it on their aggregator and whenever there is change, it will show. Then it is as simple as zapping to the one that is showing activity and participating is possible.

It is not only that advertisers want to advertise on blogs because they know they attract a lot of participants. For example, Google's content based AdSense advertising methods works seamlessly with blogs. Those who start blogs could easily make money from the ads, because the possibility of a click through is high. Consequently, since it does not cost anything to start a blog if webmasters have the time that is one way of marketing a business. If managing a blog might not be easy or handy for some reasons, since it is important, especially big businesses that do not have in-house staff to do it, they could hire outside help, because there are small agencies that can take a blog from the inception to putting fresh material on a regular basis, and to moderating the blog on an going basis.

It is one of those things that has caught up already, but for now not many blogers make money. The main use of a blog used to be simply to create a network of bloggers who exchange views about anything, from a personal diary to musing on specific topics that are hobby oriented. Bloggers can talk about anything they like and in most cases if they step over the line there are moderators that will intervene, where either the blogger can be barred or some kind of editing could take place in real time. But now it has become possible for individual bloggers to make money as there are sites that pay money for different kind of services from bloggers.

There are some who are trying to capitalize on this new phenomenon where anyone can participate and chip in a comment, suggestion, criticism, personal opinion, expertise, and so on. The key as usual is the number of participants converted into prospects to buy services and products. When the number of the participant of a given blog reaches a certain critical mass, there are businesses that want to advertise their ware on the blog with the hope that some of the bloggers will be interested in what they are offering. And for rendering the service, which could be a per-click-through payment or a commission on a closed sale, pay-per-performance, the owner of the blog could earn money.

The key here as usual is the number of participants and there has to be something good going on to attract a big number of visitors on a daily basis. Creating some kind of interest that will attract people to participate on a regular basis does that. The number of blogs that are showing any kind of success rate are very few, but the potential is there. Once the size of traffic starts getting higher, like an average of 100 visitors on a daily basis, there are advertisers that will take interest in working with the blog.

One of the earliest pioneers that saw the potential of blogs or that wanted to make blogging worthwhile was AdSense, introduced by Google. One interesting thing to take a note of about Google here is, as one of the major search engines, there are a few things webmasters are advised to do in order to get quick indexing and a good page rank in Google's search result. One of them is to start blogging using Google's Blogger format or any other site that accommodate blogging. It is evident that it definitely speeds up the indexing process reducing it to days or weeks instead of the few months it could take. Moreover, what is known as power linking can also be put to work in order to create an incoming link, a measuring rod Google and the other search engines are using to rank sites.

That aside, what the AdSense does is put ads on the blog that have relevance with the content of the blog and for every click through by visitors, the advertisers pay money to Google and Google shares that money with the bloggers. Even if AdSense is popular, the money generated in most cases is just a pocket change to cover for the minor Internet related expenses like ISP costs and the like. However, for those who have a high number of traffic, whose number is not high, the potential is there to make money with the AdSense program.

There are a few things that have to go hand-in-hand in order to make AdSense worthwhile. According to some experts high traffic, high paying ads, content that can generate high paying ads, the design of the blog itself in relation to how the ads are placed around, and how easily navigable the blog is make a big difference. In most cases, as long as there is a high volume of traffic, the most difficult part of the job is complete, but with the same token, it requires exerting some effort to attract the high paying ads. What this means is if bloggers want to make money, they will have to do things at a pro level, and they have to go out and find out what has interest and demand out there.

This will create two or even more kinds of blogging styles and it depends on individuals which one to choose, because since blogs have become so popular, and when they were started no one per se intended them to be income generators, it would mean that their generic nature should not be trampled upon. Yet, the fact that those who had seen the potential of making money on blogs have ushered the second generation of blogs should not be overlooked either.

There are a few things to be familiar with before applying for AdSense program and those requirement could be accessed form the AdSense site, but to touch on them here, the key issue is traffic, which means blogs have to stay a few months until they generate enough traffic before they apply, otherwise Google will decline them. In addition, the AdSense program is not allowed for personal blogs of any nature, which means the blog has to deal with a given niche market that is suitable for advertisers. This clearly draws a line and it only deals with the new generation of blogs or the AdSense program is deliberately rearing blogs that are pro in their content.

AdSense is not the only one that is facilitating blogs to make money. There is another program called blogads.com that will find advertisers on behalf of bloggers and what it will cost to work with them is they take a portion of the revenue, 30 percent to be exact, which is a fair deal because they do all the legwork. What is required is to become a member of the network, which requires a recommendation by another member.

Another program worth looking at, not only for blogs, but for any site that wants to generate ad revenue is adbrite com. After joining the program they advertise the blog site for advertisers, and if advertisers are interested in what they see, they will advertise on the blog in a form of a text, and they get 25 percent of what is generated.

Another similar program is offered by fastclick.com and it is more or less similar with the above, with one minor exception of a 35 percent take, and blogads.com, amazon.com, are other programs with similar offers worth visiting. What this shows is even if the work involved will be phenomenally high when compared with the bloggers that are doing it for fun or as a hobby, where a good number of hours will have to be put in as any good paying job, the opportunity of making money is there.

There is one individual known in the blog circuit for making good living from blogging and hires others to write for him. He ran four fairly popular blogs through what is known as Gawker Media and his name is Nick Denton, a facinating individual who had been up and down, and he is cited as one of the few individuals who had managed to make blogs generate money, even if it is not that much by any standard. At least he manages to pay a $2,000 a month salary for the individuals he hires to write the blog for him. The four blogs, Gawker (gossip), Gizmodo (gadgets), Fleshbot (adult), and Wonkette (politics) are worth visiting to see how the new generations of blogs are striving to make money from their blogs.

Aside from what is touched on, affiliate programs come next in generating income where putting ads of businesses that will pay by pay-per-performance basis in most cases, where if a clicking through customer on a banner, text, or button ads placed on the blog site buys a product the sellers pay commission. Even if it is a tired method, there are some that are making money on it, and as anything else it depends on the volume of traffic and the percentage of the commission is high in some cases.

Another way of generating money from blogging is by placing a donation tip jar on a site and for those who are advocating a cause, this is a good way of doing something worthwhile for the cause they uphold. There is one famous individual who is generating up to $80,000 through fundraising just from donation only. His name is Andrew Sullivan. The individual writes on varied subjects and anyone who likes what he is writing about, and wants to support the site andrewsullivan.com to continue doing what it is doing is asked to donate between $20- $50 and the outcome shows many people donate.

Again this shows that all depends on the individual's creativity to make a blog generate money in a time like this where the Internet is inundated with information. What makes the difference is packaging, putting useful, and needed information in one place where people are willing to come and get it, interact, and have their say too. Nevertheless, it requires much higher effort than the ordinary, where hobbyists are musing and having fun, while at the same time building a network. It might require taking it as a full time job.

Press Release

Press release is different because it comes into the picture whenever there is something new in case of an existing business. But for a new business it is another way of making a big buzz, because its effect is very much different from any of the other tools we discussed so far. The main targets for a press release are the media outlets and literally, they feed on press release. Most of the news coverage that they are writing about concerning new businesses or products are first instigated through press release, which means it is the business that will tell the publications what they are doing with the hope that they will talk about it in their publications or broadcasts. That will open a big floodgate for any business, because most of the reputable media outlets have a huge audience that literally awaits on them, and if a business gets a coverage in an upscale publication like Business Week or any other business publications at the same level and it is an unknown, it will raise an eyebrow. Of course, the next thing could be a visit to the site, right off the publication to see what is involved. If the business has what it takes most people could do business with it right there or they would take a mind note.

As a result, a press release is effective to cut through the chase, while at the same time if a business has an opt-in list or a purchased or rented one, it is possible to send a press release telling them the new introduction in the case of established business or if it is a startup and believes it has what it takes there is no reason why people should not know about the arrival of a new business. After all, if a business does not have something to offer it will not go into business in the first place. Even if the advertising channels are available, most of them have an earmarked price, and the judgement rests with the entrepreneur what routes to utilize, because some of them might not be worthwhile.

And if we come to think of it, there are not many things that would not raise interest in people. But there might be exceptions, like for example, a used car dealer will be better off by not trying those that are high income earners that could be reached through some of the publications, because those groups are known to buy brand new cars for the most part since they can afford it. They do not pay the price out front most of the time, and why would they buy used cars knowing all the problems related with them.

The same applies to those who sell luxury cars and if they go into mass marketing they will be wasting their money, because those who can buy luxury cars for example, could be reached through different publications these kinds of individuals are reading, but not the ordinary Joe who might be a good customer for the used car dealers. Any ad money spent on the wrong medium could be a waste of resources, which means it is up to the webmaster to visualize where and how to find his or her prospective customers.

A business selling cosmetics should be selective somehow while advertising because you might have encountered such kind of mass marketing ads reaching your mailbox. Even if most men have the significant others in their life, when it comes to choosing cosmetics they will definitely be at a loss, and if such ad is targeted at males, it is not difficult to imagine the amount of waste that will be involved. This specially makes sense in press release, because there are publications that will be happy to receive cosmetics press release because the publication's targeted audience could be females, and they will love to bring new products or services to their readers, but there are many publications that will be uncomfortable for receiving such a press release, although no harm is done. When the number of these kinds of out of whack press releases reaches the wrong hand, it is possible to feel the expense pinch.

What this shows is press release could be a targeted ad campaign than the rest of it. A newsletter could have different sections to deal with different products or sectors of the community. Those who receive the publication will know which one to give a better attention, therefore, the trick will be to create as many sections as possible. Direct sales pitch also could suffer from the same problem, but there is no harm done, either they will toss them out or delete them, and the expense is part of doing business. But if the targeted audience is known in advance the catering should be done through mediums that deal with the targeted audience so that it will be more effective cost-wise and the acceptance of the ad by the audience could also be more.

Banner Ads

Banner ads are good to promote a particular brand, because even within that split second, it is possible to be curious about what the banner is all about. If people keep seeing the banner ad whether it is static or a popup without their knowing it, they will become familiar with the brand. One day when they want similar brands chances are they will remember the brand and go directly to the site or while doing the search if they see that company carrying that brand they will somehow want to click on it, because they were seeing it many times. That itself tells them that the business could be in a good standing for doing uninterrupted business for all the while they were encountering its ad. That is why businesses would like to pay any amount of money for domains parked by others, especially if it is easy to remember.

If someone is selling computer related books, names like "computerbooks.com" says what he or she is doing. And when someone does a search wanting to buy books about computer, it is possible that this site could pop up either on the generic search result or on the paid ad, because the probability is it could be using a keyword that has computer and books. Even more, it is easy to remember "computerbooks.com" when someone wants to buy computer related books and they could make it straight to the site. But the fact that these are two words connected together might make it difficult for the search engines to read it and they do not for top results but they will get to it. Yet, it is easy to remember by those who had been encountering the ad frequently. Using www.book.com if it is available will at least make it easier for the site to pop up when searchers are looking for books of any kind, and if its specialty is computer book all that is required is to mention that in the text. When they are together and if someone is searching for a computer book, the site will be among those that could finish on top.

As far as bringing in customers through banner ad is concerned, the number is not that promising, because for every 1000 impression the buying rate is between three and six prospects, which is not high. That is the reason why banners are designated for brand promotion, which means if starting out webmasters start using banners and if they do not see the kind of result they are expecting, that is the reality, and if they do not have a brand to promote they are better off to keep away from them. Banner do not even work that great for affiliates, and the advertisers, more or less, know that when they make a deal with them, but what they want is the exposure on as many sites as possible, which is not going to cost them anything. Successful affiliates start their own web site carrying most of the product they are selling and it is these sites they promote aggressively. It should have all the bells and whistles that we were talking about to be a successful web site or a business.

As a matter of fact speaking, one of the hot businesses around is selling someone else's product, because the affiliate arrangement could be made with the business and visitors do not have to know whether they are dealing with an affiliate or not. For the most part whether when they click on the buy button or whenever they want to know more about the product they will be sent to the original seller's site through a well maintained and promoted web site. If they buy, the site they found the main seller through will get the commission.

But it does not mean there are not businesses that are selling their own products and these are entrepreneurs that come up with their own product and service, and they have to promote their business like everyone else. Their advantage is they have their own niche market that they can target and at times they too sift through a barrage of would be buyers to arrive to their niche buyers. That is what a huge email marketing accomplishes, whereas a newsletter could be reaching only those that have interest on what the site is doing and they could be converted to the niche market the site is working for. That is the difference between niche or targeted market, those who have interest in what is going on, and those prospects that could be converted into a qualified prospects. That is why there is a lot of work involved, because as we know it, people could be sitting on a lot of money not knowing what to do with it. There is no harm done in showing them the benefit they could get from doing certain things, even if it does not mean they will get benefit from every engagement they went into.

Popup Windows

Although they are irking and everyone turns them off the minute they pop up or they will install software that blocks them, they are a very good way of advertising and they work with any particular site that is willing to display them. Whenever a searcher accesses that site they pop up displaying their message. Lately they have become so fast they pop up with their message showing because who ever is behind them knows everyone is turning them off. The new popups leave an impression before they are deleted because in between the time lapse while the webmaster is turning them of, most definitely the webmaster had seen what their message is unlike the old ones which take them a while to show their content and that was why they were being slaughtered in first contact.

However, the good thing about them is when advertised with a busy site, they just keep on popping up and the number of impression could be mind boggling. They are super for brand awareness more than anything else because people are busy doing other things while these ads pop up and at times, they do not want them to obstruct what they are doing. They are much better than the static banners because these ones could grab attention.

Video Marketing

Video marketing is coming of age because of the arrival of fast Internet connection. Even if DSN is not yet the best way to view video, cable gives a clear resolution that could compete head on with TV viewing, because the digitized broadcast can travel faster since there is no congestion. However, there might be exceptions in busy areas where there will be some congestion. Congestion always interferes with the quality of the video because the quality depends on how fast and in unobstructed manner it travels to reach the outlet medium. When congestion occurs, alleviating it is costly because it is going to require the laying down of more cables, the most expensive undertaking for the cable companies, and it takes time. This means, even if it is not a widespread problem those who live in a densely populated area could suffer this malice, which means video will cease to be effective.

Since that is not the case yet and it might not be for the near future, because when the problem is spotted the cable companies could be working on it, jumping the band wagon might be helpful and all it takes is uploading a video that will explain what a site or a business is doing. The good thing about a video is a lot of useful material could be crammed into it and it could come close to as being at the place of business. Especially those businesses that require presentation and demonstration could use a video, which saves a lot of time and money. The traditional way of sending out sales people to cover a given area takes time, and when it is done the penetration level might not be as deep as it could be done through a web site, because most of the problems could be eliminated.

For one, prospects can watch it at their own time, in the comfort of their home or work place, without anything hurrying them to make decision. If there is need to know more it could be a matter of calling a telephone line, or there could be a direct forum or chat, or sending an email with the question is possible, and the decision to buy could be arrived at as a gradual process. Videos are very essential even for traditional advertising where mailing them is possible and again could outdo the traditional salesman who will encounter so many problems.

The prospects might not be home, even if they are, there is so much time to devote to each one of them, and within that given timeframe it is not possible to reach everyone.

The only way to beat this problem is to send a large team of sales people into a given area if there is a need to do the job quickly, and it is not difficult to imagine the expense that will be involved. Nevertheless, videos on DVDs could reach that same area with much cheaper cost earmarked to them, and because the cost of making a video is a one-time thing, sending them out repeatedly is possible. The distributing cost is similar with the distributing cost of a brochure through the mail, for example.

It was also noted that people give a higher worth for a video ad, which means it will not end up in the dustbin for the most part. Since it is using audio and video, its convincing power is much higher than other mediums. It is not only that a survey has found out that video DVDs for the most part, do not end up in the dustbin, as people would be happy to pass them around. So there is one powerful advertising medium that can deliver a whole lot of message in one format and its converting power had surpassed the traditional sales people.

Sending out video DVDs instead of brochures or sales promotion letters in a direct-mailing campaign had proven itself over time to be a much better way of grabbing the attention of consumers. According to some studies conducted watching video expedites the decision making process more than 72 percent when compared with ads on print and the number of consumers that prefer video over print is high.

The key here is the perception that is, videos are expensive to produce when compared to print and somehow that outlook will make people to see the video at some point instead of tossing it out. It is not only that people feel at ease to pass it to other people adding to the chance of its being viewed by more people. The studies reveal because videos use sight, sound, and emotion their converting rate of prospects into buyers is high and more creative material could be crammed into a video when compared to prints that could be very much limited. It is easy to make customers familiar with what is on sale before they set foot at the place of business where the service or product is on sale and the end result is dealing with a well informed customer that will require little or no attention.

Videos could also replace live demonstration and presentation by sales people to a good extent making it much easier to sell to a customer that is partially informed and anyone at the place of business could tend for such a customer, which could save the business money and time on closing sales. It is possible to do it in a large scale, whereas using sales people is not only expensive, but also it is time consuming until each area is independently covered.

The most common use for video is direct marketing where it is mailed to a targeted list, which might have a one-time cost attached to it as targeted list is expensive, but the list could be used repeatedly. Or the other alternative is to target a given general residential or business area that would not have any cost other than the delivery expense, which is not that high; in fact it is similar to delivering print ads like brochures.

The other common use for video marketing is what is known as "video direct-response" where other mediums are used to advertise what the business is doing and the ad in most cases could be accompanied with a video offer to further demonstrate what the business is doing. This method is clear-cut, because the prospects are familiar and the advertisers contact them if they request for the video. The same kind of campaign could be conducted for existing customers that are on record informing them of new products and services, with all the detailed demonstration to make them familiar with the new introductions or improvements.

Overall, it is a fact that video marketing works much better than anything else, because all presentations and demonstrations are conducted via video. When used for direct marketing, the area covered and the number of prospects reached could be high resulting in attracting more business, and in most cases, a second demonstration might not be required.

The cost is proven to be lower than the other mediums when seen from the amount of sales that will be generated through such advertising method, and to bring down the cost the production could be done in-house, requiring professional help if special effects are required. For the most part, the production of the video is a one time expense, and using the video repeatedly for a long time is possible even if there are new developments, making the only recurring expense to be the video DVDs used and the cost related to the delivering process.

When we come to what is taking place online, it has the same effect, because the communicating level with the prospects is much higher and richer than text or banner ads because so many important things that cannot be crammed in the other methods of advertising could be put into a video. There is no doubt that it is becoming the best method of advertising and in the near future, especially as the video viewing capability is improving, it will slowly replace banner and text ads, or not using video for marketing purposes could mean losing business.

For now because DSL is not yet widespread, the video viewing capability might not be common place yet, and even if it is, DSL is not fast enough for delivering quality video content. Cable is better, but as the number of users of a given neighborhood increases it could get clogged too, affecting the quality of the video until the cable providers do something about it, which obviously could take time. Consequently, the possibility of improving the quality of video watching capability is there. Streaming media is also picking up where streaming down all sorts of live entertainment and broadcast, or those saved on a server down to a computer is possible. Viewing all these contents requires a high-speed connection, which is improving as the number of households that are using DSN or cable is always on the rise.

In spite of the few setbacks, one other key development that is coming into the picture is interacting with the video ads, where advertisers have started demonstrating their products much more better than ever by using newly developed technologies. The experience of interacting video could come close to interacting with the products live, because most of the key utilities of a given product could be tried and examined by simply clicking on the video, which means it has evolved to more than watching a video like the earlier days. Prospects could do different things with the ads and the level of education they get from the ads put them in a better position to make informed decisions.

Video marketing, whether it is used offline or online has that special capability of informing the prospects much better than anything else in the marketplace currently. Because the content and the interaction could come close to as being at the location in real-time, and that is possible because so many relevant material could be crammed in one video film that could last for a long time. It is a proven method of saving money for the advertisers, because it is possible to eliminate repeat demonstrations or live presentation. In addition, there is enough proof that it has more convincing power when compared to the other methods, because it is more involving. The same is applicable for the consumers because whatever decision they make will be an informed one and most of all, they can make the decision in the comfort of their own home or work place, which is free of any kind of unwarranted external pressure.

RSS

RSS has become an integral part of doing business, especially in allowing access to what is taking place on a site and in a business, for that matter, on a regular basis with no ongoing effort from the webmaster. Most people should know by now how RSS works, it is simply a matter of putting XML code on a server so that aggregators that created the XML codes will find it. In fact, they find it whenever the site that they relate with has made changes in its content, and that change will be relayed to those who apply for free to these aggregators to be informed when such and such site makes a change on its content.

All the webmaster has to do is to put that XML code on the site and when visitors visit the site, they will see the orange XML sign. Whey they click on it they will see the list of the handful aggregators and chances are one of the aggregators the surfer had registration with could be among them. When clicking on the icon showing the aggregator's name, it will take the surfer to the site of the aggregators. The surfer will enter the user name and the password, and when the logging is complete the aggregator site is informed that the user want the particular material to be included in his or her aggregator list. After that, whenever there is change on the site it will show up on the aggregator list they visit on a regular basis. However, in case the surfer has not registered with any aggregator it is as simple as registering with one of the aggregators on the list.

No matter how simple it sounds the purpose it serves is huge because, people do not have to surf the Internet everyday searching for the particular material they are looking for. Before doing so, all they have to do is visit their aggregator to make a request that the material that they are looking for frequently be included into their list. Then if they do not find it when they check their aggregator it might be worth their while to do a search.

Even search engines have come aware of what RSS could be doing to the number of visitors they will get daily because, a good number of them could go to their aggregators that carry their instruction to gather information on their behalf. It is possible to instruct an aggregator to gather information concerning about a given subject even if some of them might charge money for such categorized service that goes side by side with their free service. To fend off this threat, search engines have come up with what they call "personalized service" where if someone signs up for the service the search engines will keep track of what the surfer was doing on earlier visits and whenever search is done they will try to tailor it to the surfer's past experience.

For example a surfer that uses the term "car" and visits sites that sell cars on regular basis, when the surfer does searching using the keyword "car", results that deal with car servicing will take second place and those sites that deal with selling cars could come on top. In addition, if the surfer this time was looking for car servicing, all it takes is to go down to where they are. When he or she visits next time that will be included in the search result getting priority. On another visit if the surfer wants to visit part suppliers, those ads will not be at top but they will be somewhere among the results. What this shows is the search engines are trying to keep customers that they are losing for RSS, but their success rate is lukewarm, yet some of them have their own aggregators, like Yahoo has its "my Yahoo".

In today's cyber-age, there are few businesses that do not have a cyber presence. Whether they are promoting their brick-and-mortar business, or they are a stand-alone Internet business, they have to have a web site to promote their wares and services. In addition, buyers have to find the web site in order to do business with the company. With billions of sites out there, how are buyers going to find these numerous business web sites?

One sure way is to advertise and there are what are known as pay-per-click or cost-per-click advertising methods, which are believed to be effective vehicles for advertising, but the number of businesses that are using them could be in the thousands. The question is, how could differentiating between all these advertisers is possible so that they will get fair advertising time for the keywords they have paid for? Considering that the number of advertisers paying for similar keywords are high there has to be some method to give everyone what they are willing to pay for. That is why they introduced bidding, and even if it is effective, it is very expensive in some cases.

Paying $5.00 or $10.00 for a click might not make economic sense when those who are clicking through are not buying. Even if they buy it will take a high margin of sale to offset the expense incurred. So, what is the other alternative? It is proven to be going the generic route, and with the right kind of web site optimization there is a strong belief that it is possible to attain similar result, even if this outlook is disputed to some extent.

Search engine optimization (SEO) by itself is a broad subject and at times to attain an effective result, expert help could be required. What it is dealing with generally is the making of a web site friendly for visiting search engines whenever they send out their robots. They do that once a month in most cases. However, if they are made to make the visit frequently the site will attain a higher rank, which means it has a better chance of being shown in the top-ten results, which is the ideal spot even if, at times, being included in the top-100 sites might make a difference.

The search engines have their own algorithms to follow that no outsider has a knowledge of, but those who are involved in SEO will always try to outguess new introductions so that they can implement them to their clients' web sites. At times, the search engines themselves give hints about what web sites should do in order to get a good rank.

One of the key things that the search engines like is content. If there is a lot of content, especially that will change frequently, in order to update their records they will send out their robots, at times in a daily basis or several times a day. And any site that could muster this feat will certainly end up getting a good rank, yet there are other things that have to go hand-in-hand with content in order to give a site a good rank. However, content is said to be the winning formula, simply because the search engines themselves want to present good-value sites to their searchers.

That is why blogs are becoming very popular, because so many different things could be put on blogs on a daily basis, and it is not only that, with the right combination it is also possible to attract participants. What the site owner has to do is always link the main web site that is selling or promoting the product or service with the blog so that those who visit the blog will also have a chance to visit the web site where all the wares and services are displayed. This will create power linking, which are incoming links created on purpose so that the robots will encounter them. This by itself is one essential part of SEO that we will discuss on another article, but incoming links are the other important elements search engines rely on to rank a site.

Consequently, what having a blog going means is, bringing out the robot as often as it is possible to change the content of the blog, and the way the search engines find out the change it through RSS. Rich Site Summary is a way of telling others that have established connection with a given site through the RSS mechanism that a new content is available on a blog or on a site. And search engines have the ability to check the relevancy of the material and once they are satisfied with the content that blog will be active on their list, which will improve the rank of the blog itself, because blogs also show up in search results. It is not only that the links that are planted on the blog would lead the robots to the particular site and that will add to the incoming link of the site, which will improve the rank of the site.

We have said that the main goal of the web sites is to rank among the top-ten sites when searchers are using the keywords they have picked so that they will get a qualitative traffic to their site. In order to do that they have to beat the other competitors and one way of doing that is by creating a blog, although blogs have much more use than this for businesses.

Similarly, it is possible to put fresh content on a web site and the result could be similar, except that visitors cannot participate as they can easily do it on a blog. It could also change the look or genre of a site, where the ideal situation is if visitors come to the site to deal only with what is offered, whether it is a product or a service, but mixing it with a lot of content, at times, might make the sales pitch less effective, yet it could be kept on a different page, and it might be worth experimenting.

The second batch that are important for the sites are those that will subscribe for the content that is being put on a blog so that they will be informed whenever the content changes. This shows that those who will subscribe have a keen interest in what is taking place on the blog if they want to know on a regular basis about the changes made. These are captive audience converting into buyers is easy and what will do the job is the copy or the content that should explicitly inform the visitors what the benefit of buying the product or the service is.

There are also directories known as aggregators that a blog owner can apply for and once the blog is registered, whenever changes are made, the changes will show on the aggregators index. Since these aggregators indexes are visited by a big number of people, the chance of grabbing the attention of a big number of eyeballs is possible, and this is a huge exposure that does not cost the owner of the blog site any money.

Over all, even if doing business from a web site is possible, it will add to the effectiveness of the business if there is a blog site that is not cluttered with all the wares of what the business is doing. Instead, whether they are first time visitors or subscribers, it is possible to inform them on an ongoing basis about what goes on in the particular company. Moreover, the visitors have a chance to have their say, and discuss what the particular company is doing among themselves without the company itself having a direct hand in it.

The blog also avails for the company the opportunity to interact with the visitors whenever some clarification is required, and this is in addition to the promotional effort that will be undertaken by the company. It will also enable the company to find out what kind of opinion others have about what the company is involved in, and implementing measures accordingly is possible. As a conclusion, it is needless to say that companies need a blog site as another outlet to promote what they are doing, and statistics shows those who are jumping on the bandwagon are showing a substantial result.

Podcasting

Podcasting is useful when targeting those who are on the go and there is no reason why they should not be reached while they are doing other things using their handheld devices, which could be PDA, a cell phone, or the iPod that has become popular. A big number of people are downloading music or video to watch or listen while they are on the go and that is what podcasting exactly is, putting an information in a form of a podcast on a web site so that those who want it will be able to download it.

It could be audio or video and it is done through a similar process like RSS and XML file and those who are on the go could subscribe for the podcast through the aggregators they are using and the material could be there when they want it, and it is, more or less, a targeted method of reaching prospects. It works great for those that have content that could be distributed in audio or video format, and when users subscribe for those contents, marketing the business in the background is possible.

This particular channel is becoming more and more popular and it could do wonder for some businesses, like for example a site selling books could have the excerpts of the book it is selling in an audio podcast and people could download and listen to it while they travel, drive, and the like. So it is worth covering the distance as the cost is non-existent since it can be done with a PC or a laptop that is equipped with an earphone and a mike, the recording process is already in the Windows system.

The video podcast need a camcorder and it could be loaded into a computer and then uploaded to a site. All in all, those who are on the go also surf the WWW, which means they could encounter a site with a podcast and instead of reading it at the spot they might download it to listen or to look at it later. This shows the advertising channels are on the rise for those determined webmasters who want to take advantage of them.

AdSense

There is no guarantee that those who put the AdSense program on their site would get preferential treatment from Google, but all it takes is reading between the line, because those kinds of web sites are working for Google, since they are participating outlets and through them Google makes a lot of money. That is gauged from what those kind of web sites are generating and it is a substantial amount. As a result any web site that displays AdSense program should rest assured that it could get a little bit of a boost that no one will want to talk about.

For those who might be new to the AdSense program, it has nothing to do with the AdWords program that is in charge of the PPC advertising. This one puts those PPC ads on various participating sites and those sites will get paid for every click through that came through the ad they have on their site. PPC advertisers pay Google the agreed upon payment based on the rate they agreed upon, and if Google did not come up with this program, which is one of its brainchild, the ads would have been limited to the search results only, which is lucrative by itself but this one opens another venue for generating income, at the same time it opens platforms for the advertisers to show their wares.

It is not difficult to get started. All it takes is to apply and if the web site meets Google's requirements, has enough traffic, and is not very new, they will approve the application and it is a matter of putting the ad everywhere on the site. Especially those that are using the PPC program should also use this program, because it is possible to cover their cost, and some sites make a lot of money. There had been sites showing off what they had made, more than $50,000 earning a month, and there might be some that could earn more, and PPC might not cost that much for a month even for the bigger companies.

The word also is out a while ago that Google is no more alone in the world of contextual advertising and Yahoo had come out with a beta program to take its rightful place. As we know it, it was goto.com, which became Overture that Yahoo bought in 2003 that pioneered the pay-per-click ad method. AdSense and the new Yahoo Publisher Network are an extension advertising system based on what was started years back, where text ads pop up on web sites of those who have signed for such programs according to the content that is being displayed at a given time, deriving them the name "contextual advertising".

What happens is, like any ad display if a visiting customer clicks through the ads the site will make a certain amount of money even if the customer does not buy anything. Many sites had been eking money through such a system even if the money generated does not seem to be much, but the size of the visitors is the main catalyst in making a difference. If the size of the traffic of a site is high, the number of the click-through could be high too, resulting in generating reasonably good revenue.

According to various reports there is not much difference between the two programs, except that YPN is said to pay a bit higher money, which is a standard ploy of advertising where it is done to attract more customers. The fact that the YPN service is still at the beta stage is pronounced by the lack of ads that are displayed on the web sites for the obvious reason that the program is starting out and eventually both the quality and the quantity aspect of the variety of the ads are expected to pick up.

It is good news for advertisers because competition always breeds good service no matter what it does to those who are competing and it is always the one that has good offerings that will finish ahead. It is not only that competition always forces those who are competing to come up with their best in order not to fall behind, which will result in most cases in a high level of innovation. It is also known to be a good means of checking the cost of advertising, which had been on a steep rise for some time now, and the number of players among the big search engines is expected to rise as Microsoft is also in the process of coming up with its own version. This will definitely give a respite for the advertiser who must have felt the bite as they have to foot every click-through bill, which Google shares with those web sites that were able to create an outlet for the various ads.

Since YPN is a newcomer on the scene, it is only natural if it tries to capitalize on the weak points of its competitor and one of the major steps it has taken is the whole undertaking is proactive. As a new program, YPN has upped its customer service where they are taking in feed-backs enforce, while at the same time effort to reach out customers is stepped up so that many users will know its arrival on the scene.

Among the few minor disadvantages cited were the text size could still have a problem of fitting on some web sites as the ad cannot adjust according to available space on the site even if it is possible to choose various sizes on the outset by simply clicking into the YPN control panel. There is also a cited problem with the color pattern chosen for the ads because it does not work with some sites if they have similar base color, even if the color of the ad also could be chosen in advance from the same control panel. These kinds of problems, however, are part of beta programs and eventually rectifying them is possible.

If there are more things to know, the beta program is available for the U.S. users only and it is only available in English for the time being. In addition, YPN does not allow another contextual advertiser to advertise on the same page where their ads are displayed on, which would bar Google on pages they are advertising on, Google being the only contextual advertiser. This problem is easy to solve, in case web sites want to take advantage of what the two search engine giants are offering. It is possible to use different pages for both of them or using ad rotator software that are available on the Internet could solve the problem.

YPN also could enable web sites to control what kind of ads are displayed on their sites giving them control on ads originating from their competitors and the YPN program has a built in mechanism to help block up to 200 such ads from users web site. Also it is possible to choose particular categories of ads, which is not a new practice, and if strict regiment cannot be introduced, still the web sites could have ads from the general source displayed on their web site.

Even if it is not the reinvention of the wheel, competition had been the main staple of the tech companies for a long time now. We hear a lot about who is copying who or who is putting an existing concept or way of doing things to a better use to generate money for a given company, like Google did, for example, with the pay-per-click program. Google recently went on to avail books on digital format, and both Yahoo and Microsoft jumped on the wagon and very recently Amazon has also come up with its own version, simply because some of the new findings or usage are so lucrative to pass up, and if they do not take some measures it could affect their customer base.

At the end of the day, it is not only the big companies that are being benefited, the number includes the small players too who would not have any other viable means of generating income from a web site or a blog. While content producers can focus on the quality of their content, these programs will bring money to their doors, and the size of the amount of money to be made directly depends on the amount of hard work and effort put into the works.

More Advantages of AdWords and AdSense

To have the use of AdWords there is a payment involved, because the advertisers are airing their wares to their targeted prospects, and they will be found through keywords searchers typed into search engine boxes. To do that, first they have to agree to pay Google to put their ads on its site, among search results, through the keywords they choose when they sign the deal. Google does that depending on how much they are willing to pay, because there is competition out there, and sellers bid to get the top spot, even if there had never been a consistent traffic jam, where the ads are three or four per page in most cases. Alternatively, the Google AdWords system might limit the number of times a given ad appears on the search result pages.

That does not seem to be the case either, because whenever we see the ads on the right side of the search result pages, there is always room to put more ads. For those who have noticed, it does not matter how many pages the searchers go through, the ads more or less remain similar all along, in fact they are the same initial ads that will appear repeatedly. What this could reveal is there are not enough ads for every given keyword, which could be translated into there should not be bidding war, even if that is not what we hear.

The final outcome however, is that most people are satisfied with Google AdWords that has a proven track record of driving traffic to an advertising site better than anything else, and the ad is text throughout. Somehow, the days of the banner ads are waning, because of their limited nature, where they appear only on the webmasters web site, and maybe on a few others that could be affiliates.

Furthermore, if ads had remained stationary almost all sites would have been crowded, and the system would have suffered a setback. But that problem had been solved when rotating banners were introduced, which could load as many banner as needed, and give every banner a few seconds of impression so that those that are loaded on the system will appear as many times as possible in a given period. In spite of that limitation, it does not fall far behind, for example, from what Google is doing with AdWords.

Google's AdSense that always uses text gives a little bit of a twist to what banners had been doing all along, and the major difference is AdSense is text, it does not take much to download, and a good number of them could be shown on a Web page, even if there are button banners that are smaller than text. Also AdSense is content-driven when compared with banners that are handpicked and in most cases, except that they have the potential of making money for the webmaster, they do not necessarily have relevance with what the site is doing.

A site selling a car could have a banner advertising of a cloth-selling site, with the assumption that the car-buying customer could also be interested in buying clothes. But AdSense makes sure that there is relevancy and on the same site for example AdSense would end up showing ads that have car accessories or ads that have relevance to cars only. Some might see this as a limitation, but webmasters could overcome this problem by mixing both banner ads and AdSense, and this shows there is not a perfect advertising platform to meet all needs. At times, embracing a number of them might be necessary.

AdSense has another disadvantage too, in a sense that unless the content of the site changes, the ads it will generate on a regular basis will be the same, making it similar with banners, that are handpicked in almost all cases and prearranged to rotate with no precondition. Consequently, that is why AdSense can thrive on a blog site rather than on a site that could be selling any product or service, whose copy will not be changed frequently. In that sense, it is not at all different from banner ads, but with an explosive potential that would surface if the content of the site changes frequently.

For the advertisers who are using AdWords, it creates a sure outlet where they might be effective in exposing what they do and be able to generate traffic in a large scale instead of through a banner ad that will appear on a handful of sites. The sites themselves might not be easily found, unless they advertise, and what they are using could be a fixture or even rotating banners, picked only for their money generating capabilities. Moreover, it is not difficult to see that Google's advertising system has taken Internet advertising at least one notch farther than its competitors. But it is like a vehicle where it needs more things to make it work effectively, unlike banners that might do the job as long as there is traffic, and the traffic is always scarce unless effort is exerted to direct it to a given site.

What comes, among other things, to the rescue of Internet advertisers is AdWords, where as long as advertisers are willing to pay for keywords, their ads will be displayed whenever those key words are used. That will take place on Googles search engine and on other varied upscale sites among many smaller ones that are using the AdSense program, which attract millions of visitors on a daily basis, unlike banners that could appear on a handful of sites, where there are ads touting visitors to visit an advertising site, and the site itself might not have the needed traffic to accomplish even that. That is why cost-per-click advertising is so effective, as the number of sites where the ads could be appearing is totally unlimited and it could even be mind boggling, but still limited to those who are using the AdSense program. In addition, the advertising process could be controlled and tweaked as many times as necessary in a given day and the automated system reflects the new changes introduced immediately, and most of all it is cost effective in most cases.

And the other major difference is banner advertising is performance-per-click, where the clicking customer will have to buy before the site displaying the banner makes money, whereas AdSense is per-click-through only, because there are sure payers for all the click-through. The amount paid out varies, it could go up and down, and because of the bid what Google gets could also be high. However, Google could pay out a fixed amount or a percentage, and no one per se knows how it is paying, except that people get check every now and then, and the amount could go high for those who have high traffic volume, because the higher the number of the click-through, the more the captive advertisers pay. And it is no wonder if many people choose AdSense and they could be

AdWords advertisers too, which means they can even cover their AdWords expense from what they make from the AdSense program. Google itself is also selective compared to the banner advertisers, but unless that mechanism that changes the relevance on an ongoing basis is not in place, it is not productive.

There are advocates who are saying the commercial intent of Google is changing the landscape of sites, because the number of sites that are working for the AdSense program is presumably on the rise. That presumption might not stack up because, any site that is working to meet the AdSense requirement alone cannot attract traffic, because they have to offer something of attraction and value for others. However, sites that are dealing with information that has demand or those who can create that demand are having a bonanza, because visitors will come in droves for the information provided, while at the same time they have a chance to click through what captures their interest. Whether they buy or not the site displaying the ads makes a few changes that could add up.

One other subject matter that is surfacing frequently is what search engine optimizing companies (SEO) are claiming that generic optimizing is as good as or even better than using AdWords. Some people will find it difficult to come to terms with the outlook, knowing that unless someone is operating in a shoestring budget, which is the case most of the time when someone starts doing business on the Internet, because the startup cost is very low, no one wants to waddle into that uncertainty where it takes a very long time to get indexed.

Making it to the top ten sites takes eternity and for very many sites, it will not happen. Many reasons could be cited as the cause and like it was mentioned earlier if a webmaster has a problem of keeping a site fresh because of the nature of what is involved, this might be a good route to follow or mixing the two is recommended in most cases, because one might not go without the other if doing an effective business is the drive, but AdWords could sure do the job alone even if it could hit hard on the pocket book.

Ezines

Ezines are great for any site that can produce content because most of the time, they have a big network and a sizeable audience could read the material. Some of them also facilitate or allow advertising on their site and what they charge is known to be reasonable considering that they could have a big exposure, but it is like being placed on an index where some people might go through, searching for whatever it is they are looking for. In fact, indexes are the same too, both could serve as a reciprocal link even if its importance among the search engines is on a decline, yet there has to be some link in order to be considered an authority in what one is doing.

Customer Testimonials

One great way of telling would be customers about the success of a business is showing them testimonials of satisfied customers. Most testimonials include pictures so that people do not think it is fake, which is possible. Someone who knows their effectiveness might go into fabricating them. Nevertheless, when they are genuine what it means is what is on sale really works and people would think that if they part with their hard-earned money it is safe. Even if the ethics and the integrity on the Internet are high without anyone policing it full time, there are few sporadic disappointments here and there. What is good is they are few and this kind of people that are doing business on the Internet would easily be ruined if they do not keep their words, because especially with blogs, it is just a matter of time before everyone finds about them. Before the advent of blogs if a particular site is overdoing it, there were lone rangers that will start a web site telling what the crook is doing and everyone will blow it out of proportion because that is how those who are doing business on the Internet defend themselves. Citizens arrest works just fine on the Internet like anywhere else.

Offsite Advertising

Offsite advertising is also essential because what it accomplishes is the same where it will introduce or bring to the attention of would be prospects what a web site or a business is doing. One of the reasons people are avoiding it is it could be off limit for those who want to start doing something with a shoestring budget, because nothing comes cheap. Other than that, taking advantage of every possible avenue will have a payoff down the road. Putting a URL on a car for example if it can be remembered easily is much better than a telephone number and it could tell more to the onlookers about what the site is doing. That would be true if the name of the URL had been chosen carefully and if someone sees www.computerrepair.com it is easy to remember it if someone had been looking for a computer repairing shop or when the need comes some time in the future.

The rest of the entourages of online marketing, to some degree, all have a payoff depending on what kind of purposeful follow through is applied. Distributing 10,000 brochures if not very cheap would at least attract a good amount of attention. When there are certain occasions like trade shows if the money is there, coming up with 1,000 T-shirts, with the logo of a small online or offline business that has an online presence too on them, and sell it to the public without being worried too much about making profit, as long as the cost is covered will do wonders in promoting the business or the brand. While selling the T-shirt, it is possible to give out a free pen, sell or give a free mug with the company logo. Yet, such methods could start to get expensive and that is why some people prefer the online advertising only. Because even the most effective online advertising PPC is affordable by anyone that is ready to spend $100 in two to three months time. It can avail a good exposure, not to mention competing head on with others that are doing similar things. Consequently, depending on what the business is doing, sometimes mixing offline advertising might help to do business according to one's ability to foot the bill.

Payment Systems

Now let us assume that the business is up and running and the days when people had to send a check through snail mail had passed a long time ago, because there are many if not hundreds of companies that have made selling online and receiving payment in real time a breath of fresh air. One of the most effective, easiest, and reliable systems is PayPal that is very easy to start. It only requires having a bank account or a credit card to get verification. After that anyone buying from any web site either can make the payment directly to PayPal, where the money could be withdrawn from the account attached to the PayPal account free or it could be deposited in advance, or buyers can use the major credit cards and with a nominal fee the company will process the payment on behalf of the customer with no problem at all.

There a good number of such companies around and before their coming to the scene the best way to go was to have a merchant account that used to take a long time for approval as well as a lot of money, and the whole process used to be time consuming. Still it is possible to use a merchant account depending on what kind of business is done as the smaller companies like PayPal have some limitations because it is not easy or possible to process many products at the same time, which means they are good for a small business, where the small business does not have to be worried about paying a big amount of money to the agencies that provide the merchant accounts, especially if the business is selling one or two items.

FURTHER USEFUL ASPECTS TO BE FAMILIAR WITH BEFORE CAPPING

IT UP

How well Protected Is Your System from Virus Attack?

In the age of multimedia where people are investing into buying down loaded products like music, movies, e-books and numerous software, it is very vital that these investments should be looked after from debilitating virus attacks that could be caught by simply surfing the Internet, down loading an infected material or through e-mail mostly in a form of attachment or inserts. That is, of course, when the focus is on home computers, which still could have more on their hard disks other than material that is entertainment oriented. In addition, those who are running businesses might definitely have more useful and complicated data that will be difficult if not impossible to replace. Therefore, what is to be done? The best way out of course is to buy one of the top of the lines anti-virus software that are said to be as close as to 100 percent in detecting viruses. The problem is the sophistication of the viruses unleashed into the system is always advancing and the anti-virus software needs updating in a regular basis.

Being versed with these viruses is also recommended so that whenever a new one is circulating into the system a timely preventive action could be taken. Hence, it is helpful to touch on what really viruses are and how they came into existence. We might have to go some years back, maybe as back as 1981, a period the number of programmers was on the rise, and most of the programming research was taking place in university campuses. According to some sources, there used to be games that were created to fight each other on a system and the intent was simply intellectual exercise or prank among those who were savvy in programming. Some of these activities might have instigated the coming into existence of viruses that have somehow unintentionally spread into other computers and might have done unintended things, but no matter what, there was no system that would have propelled them to spread outside of the campuses. Yet, there was an incident that could have been a rare exception where someone had tried to modify the Apple diskette and that effort had somehow spread among the community of Apple computer users.

The year 1989 brought into the picture a big behemoth like IBM and it became the first provider of anti various products to its large customer base. Most probably that might have been the turning point in the history of virus writing, as the amateur and prankish programmers changed their forms into real hackers for numerous reasons that might be time consuming to speculate on. On the wake of that, a new virus types were unleashed and they were different not only because they arrived encrypted but a decrypter which can take many forms was attached to it making it difficult for all anti virus software vendors to come up with the right algorithms to detect it, as there were few even before IBM jumped into the foray. And as it is obvious, this new development was directed to challenge the vendors who were out to retard the advancement of those whom they labeled as hackers and the nature of the game started changing, and probably set a precedent for what is taking place in today's world where big business and systems like the Internet and their dependants are made to be the main targets. The sophistication of the virus authoring methods escalated and new more damaging ones were unleashed, which were said to be deadly because they could affect back up files too, which were supposed to be the last resort in the clean up process once the other files are corrupted. Another advanced level was reached when it was possible crashing a computer.

If there is a lesson to be learned about viruses, it is that they are entities that started out with good intent and maybe advanced into a prank among some groups that definitely did not know they will be harmful, and their being harmful was realized when they started running amuck. Eventually, users started to be affected and especially businesses were vulnerable as they might have a hard time of losing sensitive records or research material that might have taken years, as it was one of the causes which necessitated the coming up of antivirus products. Then, of course, it is history as we know it, as there had come to be two camps that had been at each other's throats ever since. Aggregately, according to a source, there had been up to 54,000 viruses that had been unleashed into the wild till date, and because most of top of the line antivirus products are capable of detecting up to 100 percent of the existing viruses and the problem had been contained to a satisfactory extent. Nevertheless, when a virus is running amuck, definitely, until it is contained it could inflict a lot of damage. Moreover, the effort from the side of the hackers is not at all dying down as there are a good number of viruses that are let out into the wild.

Now, we know at least enough how these malicious creatures came into being, and furthermore knowing their different nature and what they are capable of mustering will help to keep them at bay. To quote the popular meaning of a virus that was articulated by a renowned expert on the field, "It is a program that can infect other computer programs by modifying them in such a way as to include a (possibly evolved) copy of itself". There you have it. Although not everyone agrees with what it means, what it generally means is these malicious (not always) programs will somehow find their way into your computer and could take control and make your computer do what they want it to do, that is the authors. That translates into if they want to delete files they can do it. If they want to crash your computer, they can do it. If they want to alter a program, they can do it. They have gone as far as planting what are known as Trojan Horses, which are capable of selecting particular documents out of a given system and e-mail them out to the e-mail addresses that are available on record like inside of Windows Messenger, who could be competitors and what not.

In addition, their damage is more serious in a business environment where records are so essential not to mention valuable research material, and, of course, in the age of e-commerce there is nothing devastating as having a system down. Others to be aware of are known as 'worms' and there are two kinds according to various sources, a host, and a network one. The host one stays on the host computer and once it transformed itself into a network worm by launching its copy into another computer, it is possible that it could self-distract. However, the ones that will start replicating themselves into the network will keep on carrying out what the author intended for them.

As being versed requires much more than we have covered, we have to keep digging our heels more, so that we will be more comfortable with most of the inner works of the viruses without being experts on them, as that particular aspect has a steep learning curve. Now, let us look at what they generally target. The first ones, of course, are files and these types of viruses are FILE INFECTORS. What they do is they attach themselves to program files like COMs, EXEs, BATs, OBJs, SYSs and the like and could do numerous things like changing the COM files into EXE files or executing their own payload instead of the normal program and hiding the effect so that it will not be traced. We have come across viruses that infect backup files like the Dark Avenger earlier and the source code files are not immune either even if they are in their compiled form.

The other area that is vulnerable to attack is the boot sector, as crippling it would mean to render the machine useless. Then, simply taking the latest figure on viruses will reveal that there could be if not 54,000 kinds of capabilities, there are a good number of them. Some have expressive names like stealth virus, because they can hide the damage or the change they had made on a given program, or a companion virus which is capable of replacing the existing programs by a new ones and it will be very difficult to detect what took place unless of course armed with the latest anti virus software. The list includes cavity virus which attacks sections which make sense only for programmers that are known as nulls, armored virus which is wrapped with all the tricks to make analyzing or disassembling it difficult and the list goes on.

What will be appropriate next in our pursuit of the malicious creatures is knowing their current exact state even if all it will take to fend them off is to have a good anti-virus product installed, which will be covering further ahead on how to get a reliable one. Yet, since the sophistication of the authors of the numerous viruses is accelerating at an alarming speed, a given year will have a good number of viruses that will definitely necessitate upgrading. However, being familiar with their general nature could always preempt what measures to take once they are detected or if there is news about their breaking out of the zoo or are unleashed by menacing hackers. According to a report, there were two main categories of viruses, those that gained notoriety simply because of the techniques they applied and those that have exploited weaknesses in the system and had inflicted considerable damages.

There is no sign, of course, that this endeavor will relent in the future, as all signs are predicting that the sophistication will escalate. When seen from the point of view of people who are not experts on the computer programming languages, it seems that all the possibilities must be charted and it is like a closed circuit scenario where the hackers' next move could, more or less, be anticipated, with few exceptions where there will be some who will always have a surprise under their sleeves. That will clearly attest to the fact that it does not take much of reading between the lines as to what the motives of the hackers are. The first one will probably be to outwit each other that is among the so-called computer experts and, of course, at times to disrupt business. Since the possibility of being pinned down is always there, the chance that the tug of war will evolve into blackmail and the like will be remote that is as long as the hackers do not become unbeatable.

In the meantime, what users should do is arm their system with the latest antivirus software, which are available in good number. The criteria to choose depend on the buyers' need. What seems to be important is to have one of these programs installed to feel safe to a good extent and if there are essential documents, it is advised to keep them away from the my computer area on your desk top, since it is from there the snatching and sending them sprawling into the unknown had been taking place. Other than that, if you believe that more fortification of your system is required all you have to do is throw in a firewall software that will erect an invisible barrier between your computer and the Internet and blocks any access to your internal systems without your authorization.

Distinguishing between Spywares and Viruses

Spywares and viruses are similar in their nature since both are unwelcome installations that will take place without the consent and knowledge of computer owners. However, what they do is totally different. Spywares are planted on a computer in order to keep track of what the owner is doing so that the information could be aggregated and passed on to a third party that will use it to target the owner of the infested computer with commercial pitches mostly in a form of pop-up advertising.

In the final outcome, there is no harm done except that it is a direct invasion of privacy that could get harmful if used inappropriately. Sensitive information such as credit card numbers, bank accounts, passwords for bank accounts, and emails the owner might be using are all accessible through the spyware software that could sit in the background, coming to life when the computer starts. The content of emails or any other sensitive documents could also be accessed, copied, and passed to a third party that can do anything he or she wants to do with it.

The end result is spyware software creates unprecedented access to anyone's private or business computer and can make and break the owner at will. The existence of spyware software by itself makes everyone vulnerable to a big number of abuses, even if till date, in most cases, spyware software were used only to track the buying habit of users so that a tailor-made ad will be channeled to them directly, but the possibility of changing the nature of the tracking is out there, the reason why users are scared out of their senses.

Virus on the other hand is a harmful software that could be downloaded through email in a form of attachment –that is why most people have dread toward attachments—and it could do a lot of malicious things to a computer. One of their special characteristic is they are created to duplicate themselves so that they can infest a big number of computers in order to disrupt what they are doing.

Sometimes, it is possible to encounter or catch a virus by simply surfing the Internet and from visiting other sites that are already infected. The outcome in most cases is the computers infected will be unable to function normally and the effect is more pronounced on computers used for business purpose where whatever service is being rendered could be made unavailable for users, and the disruption could cost a lot of money to companies, and in some cases they could even lose customers.

The good news, however, is it is possible to keep all of them at bay to a good extent by using various software that are out in the marketplace to do the job. Some of them tackle only virus where either they protect the computer from being infected or they will hunt the virus down after it is planted and they will uninstall or remove it. It is not, nonetheless, a 100 percent guaranty even if it is better than surfing the Internet without the protection. The other handicap of the software is they have to be upgraded on a regular basis to up their capability to the complicated level of viruses that are unleashed on a regular basis by the big number of pranksters who have taken it as a way of life, and the sophistication is always on the rise.

The same procedure could also be applied to the spyware software where it could either be prevented from installing itself on a computer or once it is installed it could be hunted down and rooted out even if some of them are known to be difficult to remove and could be get rid of only by installing the whole program again after deleting the whole content.

If this procedure is the only resort using a backup system to save some of the essential documents, if not programs might be required.

Among viruses there are Trojans and worms, and Trojans are exactly like their name where their declared purpose and what they do is not the same. They could tell the user that they will serve a given useful purpose, but once they are installed they will resort to what their creator intended for them and in most cases they do not duplicate themselves like viruses. However, worms are more or less viruses that can replicate and attach themselves with various outgoing documents and applications on the host computer.

When it comes to spyware there are several varieties to be aware of and one of them is "adware" whose sole purpose is to display pop-up advertisements in most cases that are already implanted in the program according to the surfing habit of the users.

The other kind is "trackware" which has the capacity of tracking everything the user is doing on the Internet and that information could be used for targeting ads for the user that is if it is not used for any other damaging purpose like stealing credit card information or bank account number, and passwords.

There is also what is known as a "tracker" and what it does is keep record of every keystroke in a special file and send that file periodically to the hackers, which could enable them to do all sort of damage both on personal computers, and on those that are used for business with sensitive customer information. One of the major problems cited is when a computer is infected with all these barrages of spyware software that are executing numerous instructions in the background, they will definitely hamper the performance of any computer bringing it down to a crawling stage, and that is when users will find out that their system had been infected severely.

On top of all these, these kinds of software are known to do other things like hijacking affiliate payments by redirecting the click that is coming from the affiliate sites to the hacker's site.

What this shows is the vulnerability level of surfing the Internet or doing business on the Internet is on the rise. Yet, there are products that are coming to the rescue of Internet users and some of them boast a 100 percent protection. Nevertheless, to get that out of their product regular updating is required, which does not come free in most cases. There are also freeware software out there that promise to do the job even if they might not be as good as those that are charging for it.

Other known products to be aware of are Ad-Aware and Spybot-Search and Destroy, which are free to download. Among the well known commercial products Symantec, McAfee, and Sophos are known to be the best, and they bundle both anti-spyware and anti-virus products, even if they have to be updated regularly to be effective.

A lot of precaution has to be taken when using these kinds of products because their claiming to be anit-spyware or anti-virus is not enough as a good number of them had been themselves spywares and viruses, and that is why, at times, it is important to stick with the household-name products.

There are sources who say avoiding using Internet Explorer might help to keep these malwares at bay, yet even if there are few browsers out there, they might not be as good as IE, which is known to come up with security measures and patch-ups on a regular basis to make its usage safe. All in all, it is very important to become aware, which products are out there affecting computers, and passing out information for a third-party hackers who are in a position to use them for whatever purpose they choose to.

A recent virus that was in circulation was Kama Sutra, the name it was using among many other names. It also had names like W32/Nyxem-D worm, Grew.A, Blackworm, and a few more. Reports had said at the time it was causing damage that it was different from other worms because it was not doing what it was doing to get financial benefit, as some of the other worms are known to be driven by such motivation for wreaking havoc. Kama Sutra was said to be deadly because it hunts and deletes Word, Excel, Access, and PowerPoint documents, PDF, including the Adobe PhotoShop, Zip files, and many more from the hard drives of computers that are infected by the virus.

It is not different form many of the worms that activate themselves when opening email attachments, and it uses exotic pornographic enticements to make the victims open their attachments. The few of the exotic terms it used were Crazy Illegal Sex, Give Me a kiss, Miss Lebanon 2006, and School Girl Fantasies Gone Bad. The first thing it did was disable any anti-virus or firewall software that is running on a given computer and will take the usual route of worms where it will start replicating itself by sending out emails to all email addresses that it finds in the address book of the infected computers. This one at least does not open backdoors so that intruders can take control of computers.

What this shows is on a given month, up to 20 to 30 viruses could be unleashed doing all sort of malicious things to computers that they infected. According to reports about the breaking down of virus activities for the year 2005, 42 percent were Trojans, 26 percent were bots, 11 percent were backdoor Trojans, 8 percent were dialers, 6 percent were worms, and 3 percent were type of adware/spyware.

However, in spite of the nuisance and damage they can cause, their main way of activating their malice is when opening attachments. By now, almost everyone knows that it is almost breaking a taboo to tamper with attachments that should be deleted immediately and thrown out, even out of the recycle bin so that they do not explode in there because some of them are time bombs. Yet, still there are individuals that have to exchange these attachments to circulate material and information, and there are a number of suggestions.

One of them is never to open an attachment from an unknown source; even some go as far as saying that not opening attachments even from a known source will reduce the chance of these malicious codes from circulating. Many users state outright that they will not accept attachments and if they receive them, they would certainly delete them and that is a highly recommended policy if it does not deter the working arrangement. In addition to that, there are experts advising not to send or receive joke files, erotica or pornography, gif files unless they are work-related, and screensavers, because all these files can have any kind of virus attached to them and when they are opened the virus will execute its own instruction and the nightmare could start.

The second important step to take is to install a firewall around the system where no material will go through without the consent of the computer owner. It is a little bit rigid and could affect the performance of the computer while the checking mechanism is executed, but it could be worth it for some that do not want to lose valuable documents on their hard drive.

Another highly recommended step to take is to install anti-virus and anti-spy software, which have the capacity to hunt and destroy viruses the minute they execute their malware on the computer they install themselves. It is a proven method of keeping viruses out of a computer, but they need updating on regular intervals. What is taking place out there in cyber space is a war among companies that are selling anti-virus, anti-spy, or firewall software and those who are determined to make their life difficult. It is not only that most of the viruses that come into existence have a motive of being benefited financially, because some of them have the capability to steal sensitive information like credit card numbers, passwords, important documents, or execute instructions to alter search results to divert landing pages, where the intruders could get paid for diverting traffic form the normal pages, but for them it is a matter of survival to outdo the anti-virus software and they always come up with new ways of getting around the existing security system.

Among the suggestions, there are some that recommend using the FireFox web browser, which they are saying has fewer vulnerabilities and holes when compared to Internet Explorer and the other popular web browsers. We should take this with a grain of salt, because the reason why it has less vulnerabilities could be it is in use less than the others, and it might not be as efficient as the others. One effective way of fighting these vulnerabilities is whenever they are spotted there will be an introduction of a patch that is available from Microsoft, for example. In case the vulnerability is on Internet Explorer, Outlook, Words, or sometimes the Windows Operating System itself, for those with the expertise, keeping a follow-up of these changes helps a lot.

Among the various good advice available out there one of them is not to click on links on emails, whose source is unknown, because there are worms that could trigger their malware through such a process. The other important advice is to back-up a system, at least the most important documents that are difficult to replace so that when something happens retrieving them is possible.

Downloading also allows viruses to cling on files and enable them to land on the downloading computer. They can execute themselves while opening the downloaded file and there is a need for precaution. There are suggestions about floppy disks being a means of spreading viruses because they could have been in an infected environment and running them through an anti-virus program before using them could reduce the risk. To make things worse even visiting infected web sites will expose surfers to infected material and the best way to protect a computer from this haphazard disaster is to install the anti-virus software.

There are many sites like Hotmail and Yahoo for example that have a built-in anti-virus system that is updated with the up to the minute new introductions that offer email service. If there is a virus they both can detect it immediately and will not allow the users to open the email, which is proven to be a very safe method of using email instead of allowing these numerous viruses to execute their malware in unregulated environment.

All in all, there are sites that keep track of these occurrences, and because their number is huge, it is only the activity of the top 20 viruses that can be tracked and they have a rank form 1 to 20 on the severity of the damage they cause and how many times they recur in a month or in a year, because some of them stay on the top of the list for a longer period and are fixtures that have to be tackled with on an ongoing basis.

What You Have to Know about Fraud

One thing to notice about fraud here is it does not come easy because there is a good amount of devising involved, which shows that it could be a full time occupation for some, or it could be something that will be picked when someone wants some windfall to come his or her way, or it could dawn on someone when he or she encounters vulnerability and getting away unscathed is perceivable. Doing it only for malicious reasons might be practical when one is novice to the field of defrauding and when attaining positive success rates is possible, the goal of the undertaking might evolve into being benefited.

Individuals who are fraud-prone might not be very successful in life when it comes to making a good living, or they could be at the prime of their career, but want to take it some notch farther by getting rich quickly or like it was mentioned earlier, any alluring vulnerability in a system could entice individuals to take advantage of it. As a result, the motive could differ from one case to the other. Now, what is daunting is the list of frauds individuals are involved in, because it could cover a big spectrum of business activities. If there is one good thing, specially in this millennium, it might be possible to put them into two categories because of the advancement of technology, which had ushered in the World Wide Web, where tantalizing types of crimes are taking place compared to the real world, which is becoming to be known as off-line and of course online, when we talk about cyber crime.

The kind of caliber applied in both cases is very high and there is no lack of ingenuity in either of them. However, if there is a problem, as mentioned earlier it is difficult to touch on all of the frauds that are possible to undertake because of the sheer size. Almost any business activity or transaction that one could be involved in could end up being a fraud. The real meaning of fraud could start from getting less for what you paid for, or to be overcharged unfairly or literally when anyone who is in a position of rendering a service or selling a product is not carrying out their duties according to what is stated in the law or based on what the conscience dictates. Selling a defective product that might have a dangerous side effect or outcome, or not rendering the service claimed or intended for and the like also fall into fraudulent engagement. In addition, if someone goes out of his or her way and plot schemes to take advantage of anyone, in any form, it is a fraud. Therefore, any deviation from the norm of doing things, especially when exchanging a service or a product for payment is involved is a fraud. Hence, just to touch on the major fraudulent activities out there that had been kept in the record, let's go through a list of incidents that were reported here and there on the various media so that at least we know what kind of form they take in real life and the list could back a few years.

- A Dr. claims $5.7 million in false medical claims to insurance companies where insurance carriers paid out about $3.2 million. Another Dr. fails to declare his income from a scheme he participated in by providing false medical claims.

- There is an incident of a man duping a blind woman who hired him to help her run an apartment building and the amount of the fraud was up to $650,000 an amount that disappeared from the woman's account.

- A lottery scam that originates in Canada which preys on seniors where they will be informed that they have won a big amount like 20 million, and they will be asked to pay tax on it in advance before they take charge of their winning as the Canadian legal system requires it.

- People involved in drug trafficking are using mortgage to launder their ill begotten money.

- There is one story from Nigeria where the defrauders claimed that someone wants to take out a big sum of money out of the country, but they need an advance to carry out the undertaking. Those who gave out money will share the loot or what ever it was going to be, which was a hoax and a fraud that caught a lot of attention and which involved a good number of people and this kind of prank appears in the email regularly.

- There was an incident where a company was using a scrap to debase precious metals so that they will weigh higher.

- Real Estate is infested with fraud as a minor mistake like signing deals in a rush, making incorrect assumptions about the deal, making mistakes by creating loopholes while drawing the deal can go a long way, or even someone might go out to defraud others.

- Counterfeit money pops up now and then and there is not much to do about it except to be careful and at times avoid the use of larger bills, even if governments are doing their to make it difficult.

- Especially for those who are in a position of hiring, there are many fake qualification papers in circulation.

- Telemarketing scam where people have to divulge personal information or buy and pay over the telephone for goods that will not be delivered.

- There are ads floating around with false claims and worse, there are times using the products could be dangerous if they have to do with health problems, like heart disease, cancer, aids, diabetes, arthritis, multiple sclerosis and others, as such individuals are willing to try anything that promises to ameliorate their situation.

- There is a wine fraud, for that matter it could involve any spirit that could claim what it is not competing with genuine ones, a fraud that is difficult to detect.

- Identity theft, which is common and will result in the defrauder doing a lot of things with it, which could cause a financial nightmare for the victim as there are incidents mentioned in some reports where the defrauders going into buying spree of expensive items such as cars, obtaining loans and credit cards. The way they get those identities could vary and some of them are worth to be aware of as they could befall anyone. Some cited examples on various reports vary from being employed in a position where people's identities could be easily stolen, to individuals who prey on newspapers obituaries, then learn surviving spouses from the funeral parlor and contacting the victims by posing as a state revenue agent to obtain information on the deceased. Also there are individuals who are in the business of fabricating and selling IDs for a sum as little as $300.

- Art fraud, charitable solicitations, credit repair scams, job listings and job search firms fraud, Odometer scam, vacation scams, smoking cures, small business scams, land sale scams, gemstone investment scams are among the many frauds that are inflicting losses on unknowing victims.

The internet is a totally different story as it requires to be savvy in programming languages to go through the mazes and achieve any kind of success rate in defrauding others in a rewarding manner. Nevertheless, there are a good number of ways through which people encounter defrauding. One of them and the most common one is a credit card fraud. Before, engaging in any criminal activity, one has to obtain the credit card number of the victim and this is where hacking is involved, and individuals with the know-how will have to go into a given system like a database of an internet based company and get away with the credit card information. Among the incidents mentioned on some reports some nationals and ethnic groups are good at this kind of scheme. And they do it for extortion. One reported incident was one of the defrauders compromised a system and something like 55,000 credit card numbers went missing. What ensued was the company got a request to pay $100,000, which it apparently ignored and 25,000 of those stolen credit card numbers were made available on a web site, which was a maximum exposure.

Another recent incident is a boy who stumbled upon an underground software that was able to retrieve e-mail addresses of people who logged into America Online chat room, and then the program will send e-mail using AOL letterhead informing the customers that their account was deleted by a system failure and if they want to continue using the service they have to register again. Consequently, of course people believed the story and cooperated without knowing someone was phising their credit card numbers. The boy for sure went into a buying binge but the damage was not devastating. And not everyone is capable of coming up with that kind of software, which would highlight the caliber of the hackers although it is difficult to put a finger on the direct motive of these kinds of engagements as that kind of capability could get a good use in the real world.

Another target is the stock exchange and this one could be anybody's cup of tea as it does not require to be savvy in anything except to have a good follow up of the stock market. Schemes known as "pump and dump" and illegal touting are playing a major role in this case. The "pump and dump" scheme used to be undertaken at a lower scale, where a few number of individuals will pump a stock among a given circle, with the hope that it will break out of that circle eventually and will spread at large. Now, because of the Internet, it could be carried out in a very large scale because once a list is obtained, which is not difficult as they are on sale, spamming will take place. In addition, there are bulletin boards where all sorts of touting messages could be posted giving the pump a maximum exposure. Then, of course, touting could also be unleashed through e-mails. The effort is to raise the price of a stock to a high level, and the defrauder should have a good position in the company's stock, which is acquired when the price was very low. Finally, if there is a price surge because of the pump and tout, the defrauder will dump all the stocks that are acquired with dirt-cheap prices and could disappear from the scene. Eventually, when the dust settles down, people will realize that the stock had been pumped and whatever touting they were inundated with was fabricated and everyone will want out, leading to the plummeting of the price of the particular stock. This is very risky at a time many people are investing online.

Another area where fraud is becoming rife is online auction and according to reports, online auction was the subject of 48 percent of the complaints received by the FBI. Other scams like securities and commodities complaints were at 16.9 percent, credit-card complaints, 4.86 percent, identity theft, 2.96 percent, business opportunities, 2.5 percent, professional services complaints, 1.2 percent, travel "scams," 0.3 percent, pyramid schemes, 0.3 percent, and check fraud .1percent. When we go into quantifying the total loss for fraud, some $700 million in online sales were lost to fraud in 2001 that latest available figure. That represented 1.14 percent of total annual online sales of $61.8 billion. Online fraud was 19 times higher than off-line frauds according to various reports. A survey of 1000 people conduct 5.2 percent said they were a victim of a credit card fraud and 1.9 percent said had suffered identity theft. Mechanisms to help people fight credit card theft, like password-based applications, public key infrastructure, smart cards, and disposable card numbers, which have received a lukewarm acceptance, are in place and are helping to contain the problem. On top of these, hacking for various purposes and virus planting are the other major criminal activities individuals are involved in online.

Other than that there are here and there new frauds sprouting, like for example around the Sept 11 incident, there were a big number of bogus e-mails asking for donation, and in the process people are asked to fill out information about their personal identity and credit card numbers. After spotting the problem people were advised to contact the Better Business Bureau to verify what they will be involved in would be genuine or not. There was also a case where some hackers were using "FBI" or "fbi.gov" letter-head in a circulated e-mail to make it look like it originated from there and it asks, "Your application is approved. Please fill out this form to confirm your identity", which will ask for all essential information, and the FBI had to come out and say that they don't ask such kind of information at all for any reason. Another hot incident was when hackers broke into a U.S. Navy computer and made off with source code that controls dozens of military and commercial satellite system. Although it is an older version, they were assessing the possible damage and were taking counter measures.

To sum it up all, going over what was reported as the frauds could give an idea with what victims in most cases were grappling with.

- The first in the list was about spams relating to the WTC.

- Identity theft.

- Nigerian letter scam.

- Viruses.

- Chain letters, those that are asking to add a name to a given position and move the same name to a different position, send a given number of this letter to friends and the like. According to the report, these kinds of activities lack legitimacy.

- Online auctions were on the list as it takes a good amount of investigation at times for any deal to go through.

- Credit Scams, from a promise to repair a credit problem, to avail affordable credit that would end up costing the unknowing victim a lot more than following the ordinary route.

- Internet Investigators, which according to the report are misleading and will end up giving out leads to Web sites that are charging for the information that is sought.

- Medical Scam with a false promise of ailment such as Herbal Viagra was one the example.

Therefore, in the real world, as there are people who are out there to earn a decent living, there are also those who want to go into defrauding others. Some will get away with it and most will end up paying a high price for attempting to acquire things easily or for trying to acquire things they are not legally entitled to.

The Digital Economy is here to Stay

The contribution of the Internet is focused on the availing of a platform and a high degree of communication tool at every level that is be it for business or at a personal level, and more or less, it was the final piece of the puzzle in the pursuit of the digitized communication. The next step was to capitalize on the readily available possibilities, as no one else had been painted into a corner for quite some time other than businesses, because they had only managed to come up with a very costly and a not very efficient means of communicating among themselves. That is without mentioning the other gold mine the advent of the Internet availed to them, which is to have a much better access to their customers.

To address the first issue, which focuses on communication among businesses, it is not very difficult to imagine what kind of time is involved in production, as simply citing one example is enough. In the auto industry, it used to take four to six years from conception to bringing a new model into the market, and according to the same report it takes the Japanese only three years. By using the Internet as a medium of communication they have reduced that to 30 months and now they want to bring down that to 20 months or more. Of course, all this is made possible because of the attaining of high level of data management and this process could be feasible only when data in whatever form it is, is converted into a digital configuration so that it could be manipulated by computers that are advancing at a neck-breaking speed. Then effective and fast communication among those who are in charge of the design and manufacturing makes a big difference. And that is where the Internet parachuted in after going through a tremendous innovation itself, from being incepted for a military use, to be modified and to be found useful to universities and scientific use, and eventually it evolved to what we know it today.

To make the Internet work, the synergy of consumer electronics manufacturers, media conglomerates, telephone companies, computer manufacturers, software companies, satellite builders, cell phone service providers, Internet service providers, television cable companies, electric utilities, participants in B2B (business to business), B2C (business to consumers) and C2C (consumer to consumer) will have somehow to come together and merge to do business. Then, of course, a good dose of marketing could bring to all involved parties what is up for grab and the wheeling and dealing secession will be ushered in.

However, we should not dampen our enthusiasm if we put a leash on it, because unless we see issues from different perspectives everything might sound like a mirage. If we start from B2B platform, the main achievement had been touched on and to expound on it, the time factor for one, of doing business among businesses had swindled down considerably. There is no more doing things manually in a constant basis or monotonously for that matter, as all data is processed and stored electronically and could be retrieved in any form when the need comes to use it. The time it takes to exchange information has come down to minutes or hours at the most. It could be e-mailed, or the involved party could log into a web site, by obtaining authorization in advance to retrieve important and sensitive documents or information that used to need extra care and much longer period to exchange. What that translates into is, any time that will be saved through effective communication will add to a faster pace of bringing products to the market, which is a central issue. As well, the possibility of saying good by to the yesteryears where weeks or even months where wasting time was involved in exchanging vital information had been achieved quite some time ago. Then, of course, one of the factors that boost productivity is simply doing things more efficiently, so that some kind of cap will be put on the time factor and the allocated cost as they have a direct impact on productivity and the profit margin.

If we try to address what takes place between B2Cs, it is, more or less, business as usual, but on a different platform and the enhancement starts from 7/12/366 capability. All it takes is to have an efficient web site on the Internet and with a good dose of marketing the rest will take care of itself. When consumers surf the Internet searching for products, services, information or entertainment the possibility of being found is there, and that problem will be eliminated for big businesses that have become household names as consumers who are aware of their Internet presence could directly log into their web site. In this kind of a situation paying attention to the effectiveness of the web site is paramount as it has a making or breaking capability. All things considered and if the customers want to part with their money, they have to be able to buy the product at the spot, of course, using their cards or the few available Internet currencies. Then the rest is routine, as people want a secured transaction to take place for all the good reasons and their goods have to be delivered on time as promised, unless the seller wants to be badmouthed, as word of mouth has the capacity of besmirching a reputation of a business.

Here, both businesses and customers have reaped some benefits. It is a second and recent outlet for businesses, which got the recognition as the click-and-mortar alternative. In addition, all businesses want is to utilize their full capacity and see those goods or services out the door in droves and this platform will definitely add to that momentum. The advantage of the Internet is like some of the other mediums such as TV. People could surf the Internet for entertainment and to do other things too like to learn about different products and providers, search for jobs, manage their finances, obtain health information or scan for news, other than that being engaged in a buying spree and an ad campaign will have a good chance of catching a big number of eyeballs as the number of people surfing the net has already surpassed the one billion limit at around the end of last year, that is 2006. That is what businesses are salivating about and luckily, there is a big payoff in it that is not yet tapped into as this could be the tip of the iceberg. Some of the advantages from the business point of view are cited to be cutting cost of purchasing, manage supplier relationship, streamline logistics and inventory, planned production and reaching new and existing customers.

In addition, there are go betweens that could be truncated benefiting both businesses and consumers. Getting rid of middlemen like salesmen, wholesalers and retailers or expensive well located outlets, all have their ramification in cutting cost and the savings will be translated into selling goods and services much cheaper, not only a bonanza to the consumers but a bait that will make them come again and again. The cost-cutting aspect of the business will embrace those in the service industry like banks, airlines, insurance, and car rental agencies too and theirs is more pronounced because the savings could be 30 to 50 percent. In all of these what the customer benefits is variety, ease of purchase and lower prices. Of course, what will be sacrificed is lack of examining the product from a close proximity, delayed time span to have the use of the product, risk of exposing one's financial status, the possibility of being duped as there is no effective policing except citizen arrest, which could arrive on the scene late, to receive a damaged product that will take a long time to exchange etc. as there are times the merits outweigh the demerits and vice versa.

However, if there is a catch, from past and recent experience, for some reason it does not work for everyone. There are some companies that have benefited greatly. Companies like Cisco Systems is talking about billions of dollar worth of business, Dell Computers, Amazon, e-bay and a handful few are also talking about a favorable business turnover. The various search engines such as Google and Yahoo need to be counted too. A company like Intel was talking $2 billions of sales every month as back as the year 2000. Yet, there are others in fact a big number of them whose sales is not picking up big-time still, and because the fundamental cause is still murky, that is why we should put a leash on our enthusiasm. The question: Is the whole issue of the Internet wrapped in unprecedented hype? It could eventually lose its teeth as the volume of business triples and quadruples, because it might be the hype that could be throwing gas at the whole issue adding to the explosion.

The Main Components of the New Economy

The hype that is surrounding the "New Economy", when it is stripped off its enigma what it will become is the outcome of years of innovation. And naturally when we innovate we have to introduce new ways of doing things and these new ways of doing things by themselves must have gone through the snail's pace transformation process and somehow, when someone started to apply them to the workplace, they have overnight become oil and fire that are near impossible to extinguish.

Attributing the whole thing to the advent of digitization is possible and digitization in its turn had been possible by the coming of age of computers. On the outset, it was of course an expensive undertaking in all its forms. The kind of huge, building and room sized machines that were available to do the computing tasks, brings to mind the space they had to occupy and the cost of procuring and maintaining them. The rest is history. Smaller and affordable desktops started sprouting from every corner and the like of Altair most probably the first small desk top in 1975, Apple in kit form in 1976 and, of course, IBM jumped into the foray in 1981. The software market that started out with Fortran in 1956 was followed by LISP and COBOL in 1958, including the original BASIC programming language around that same year, the language which supposedly had its compiler written by the like of Bill Gates and other collaborators. Eventually the industry had made it to the Windows Operating System, which had come to play a prominent role over the years and it is now said more than ninety per cent of computers are using it. When you take into consideration the fact that almost, half of the American households have more than one computer; it is not hard to imagine that the size of the market is overwhelming. In the wake of that, the computing power of these newer machines has also expounded rapidly and had made it to a lightning speed.

That is when people started to realize the advantage of digitizing all their documents because it does not only save space but it is more tidy and efficient compared to the clumsiness of the paper shuffling and paper chasing era. That, of course, was a humble beginning and everyone held the momentum and efficiency obtained in high regard. In addition, eventually word processing and seeing all or most of company documents digitized were not enough. Businesses like Oracle, SAS and People Soft started to pump the market with dazzling products that have proven to be doing better and efficient jobs than their human counterparts, in handling and follow up of Customer Relation Management (CRM) and Product Data Management (PDM) or its latest version Product Lifecycle Management (PLM) and many other indispensable functions like sophisticated data base management. Business owners have attested to the fact that these kinds of products haven't only reduced the man-hour time it used to take to oversee these operations, but they have admitted loudly that they have cut cost too.

Now, guess who has emerged as the dominating figure in all this tribulation, of course it is known as IT and as we all know it, it stands for Information Technology and the fact that it is a bit mind twisting is undeniable. Before IT became a household name, technologies like CAD (Computer Assisted Design), CAM (Computer Assisted Manufacturing) CAE (Computer Assisted Engineering) were in the picture since the 1970s and were doing wonders without being so audacious and if one wants to talk about innovation what CAD/CAM and CAE ushered in is almost a revolution by any standard. Moreover, it was possible to inundate the medical and scientific fields including high level researchers in numerous fields with a myriad avalanche of software products. Sources name more than 400+ software aimed at the medical field alone from about 50+ publisher. The same goes in almost every field. Yet, this newer version of innovation that started out by digitizing documents, then succeeded in facilitating the clumsy nature of the day-to-day work place, by equipping it with the like of word processing, record keeping and retrieving mechanisms like database is emulating to have the upper hand. There is more to it though as it is flanked by a promise to change the tedious nature of the follow up process of bringing whatever is produced to the consumers or the dealing or interacting with the suppliers in a more efficient, timely, and economical way. It is proven time and again that there is some verity in it and there is no better place than getting that verity straight from the horse's mouth, as it is the top management in most businesses that are attesting to these facts and of course the media is taking their word for it.

Moreover, what is throwing oil at the fire is the advent of another technology that is said to be still evolving to make it where every visionary wants it to be and it is the Internet. There is nothing wrong with it as it is a marvel of our time, and doing some research on it will unravel all the good things it is doing, and of course, its shortcomings will surface too. However, for our purpose here, this whole issue is out of proportion. Most of all, what the advent of the Internet promised was to avail among many things a badly needed platform to conduct business electronically where "brick and mortars" will be transformed into "click and mortars". Instead, the whole undertaking resulted in ushering the era of the dot-coms and e-commerce, with all the bubble and excitement they created in the stock market, which had somehow subsided after the burst of the bubble where most of the dot-coms, of course, had bitten the dust. Some had benefited greatly and some got the burn badly, while some had to bite the bullet. Since almost all of it was speculation, the outcome does not surprise anyone, as it would have had the reverse effect if some kind of success were attainable.

For those who are supposed to be coming in from the cold as the "old economy" is being made to look like, the highly talked about new factors are simply parts of the innovation process, and the modern era had never been caught sitting on its hands. Realizing this fact might save the whole undertaking from following the dot-coms' footstep. The quality issue had always been on the minds and agendas of every one, although except experimenting, a 100 percent certainty as to what direction the aggregate effort will take might have not been feasible. Touching on the "quality of capital" issue in the "New Economy" could be tricky, because the focus is tilted badly towards one sector only. And those who are coming up with new ideas that could be backed with a software, like Microsoft and many others are doing, will end up being the champions, not to mention what they stand to reap as a reward. But the fact that these entities are laboring in the majority cases, to facilitate the works or lives of those who are either in charge of the "brick and mortars" or those who are eking their living by being employed by them should not elude everyone. As well, the fact that these "knowledge management" tools are benefiting and helping the whole industry move forward is undeniable, but since the achievement and progress attained is inter-linked and interdependent with technology, the fallacy of being one sided should be kept on alert watch.

The same applies to the "quality of labor" in the modern work place where innovation has left no stone unturned. The old ways of doing things are definitely giving way to the new wave of doing things and this will require a constant or a lifetime learning, which is said to be costly in whichever way it is looked at. At any age, if employees want to keep their competitive edge, they have to catch up with the new technologies that will be pushed at them from the so called innovators, who might not run out of steam for a long time to come. And the expense issue has become a no-brainer where at times the employees themselves have to fork it out or if they are lucky enough they will see their employers sneezing it.

All in all, what is certain is there is no looking back and coming to terms with the theme of the era, which is the "quality of life" of people where in the long run what people do for a living will have to be more palatable is paramount. The ambiguity for sure is there and certainly is daunting as some have boldly come out to say people will have to use their heads only. As misleading as it may sound, it might mean delegating some of the hard works to robots that are coming to the rescue or it might mean we have to do things intelligently, that is unless it has a different connotation.

The other key factor is productivity. Because it has evolved tremendously over the years, it has definitely defied the gauge the like of the Federal Reserve officials were using, and that had been manifested no where else other than in what took place in the economy where no matter how heated it was its effects on inflation was nil, a phenomenon everyone scrambled to decipher without much success. However, finally it was possible to pin down the cause to the "high level of production" that took place because of IT. As a result Benchmarking, Effective Knowledge Management, and the implementation of a Customer Focused System had resulted in bolstering the bottom line by giving boost to ROI (Return On Investment) which is the goal of most businesses, in almost all cases.

Hence, the juggling of Applications and Knowledge Management Systems hand in hand with technology will have to come to the forefront of every business's agenda so that they will not be hamstrung from optimizing profit, the one factor which will guarantee their existence and would propel them ahead of the cut-throat competition.

It should not Cost Any Money to Do Business Online

E-commerce is poised to change the way people do business, by allowing them to wring more out of every transaction they execute. Inferring the fact that it is multi thronged is possible by stipulating who the immediate beneficiaries are. Basic economics has always had it that in almost all cases what is inflating the price of commodities is what is inputted in them in a form of labor, material, know-how, machinery, rent, transportation, marketing, and promotion and tax. Now, when e-commerce is going to be in a full swing, it will affect most of these cost-factors and the strive is going to focus on stripping them down to zero. Moreover, in the business world, be it manufacturing or service, what the business people literally do is pass these expenses to the consumers, so that they can cover their cost and realize a profit. When there is less to pass to the consumers, naturally consumers will respond positively by spending more, which has a direct effect in boosting the economy. The spiral effect will not stop there. Business will be encouraged to produce more because the lower price has created more demand, which will require hiring more people, which means more disposable income, and the overall result will be the economic boom that was observed in the 1990s.

Nevertheless, if there is a catch it is the fact that e-commerce is only emulating to make it there, and for sure it will be a while before the trek is completed. What actually is taking place now is everybody from businesses to consumers and governments are paying a very close attention to what's happening to e-commerce in general and are chipping in inputs that are keeping it going. As well, there are some businesses that are already reaping the benefit. These businesses are made up of two groups, those who are offshoots of the brick-and-mortars and those that are independently incepted to function on the Internet only, like the dot-coms that had suffered fatal causalities because of not having a solid back-up. Therefore, those who are poised to be benefited greatly in the long run are those who already are established businesses with track records and a favorable success rate and are in a form of brick-and-mortars. The fact that they accommodate themselves with e-commerce outlets will enhance their business by enabling them to reach a wider market while at the same time they can emulate to bring some of their costs down, the target being zero, and e-commerce has the potential to accommodate that.

How the aspired zero cost effect could be arrived at could vary according to the nature of each business, but certainly e-commerce has demonstrated its capability of rendering the particular feat, even if it is going to take more innovation to see its full potential blossom. If we take the cost of labor as an example, which is known to be a major expense for any business, because of IT and the introduction of new technologies, fewer individuals are becoming in a position to handle much more volume of work, allowing business owners more room to play when it comes to setting their profit ceiling. Of course, simultaneously, the expertise and the quality of labor are also being revamped in an ongoing basis and the end result is anticipated to be much enhanced outcome in a form of products or services, in a much affordable price. However, since the transmission from quantitative labor to qualitative labor is also underway, quality labor is more expensive, a culprit that might end up sapping whatever gain attained by downsizing the labor force.

If we look at technology, taking a huge stride was possible in certain areas where there is no reason why repeating is not possible in other sectors. One good example is the future of the telephone industry, which is under a threat because of what VoIP had introduced into the marketplace. The introduction had made making phone calls very cheap when compared with what customers are getting using the Public Switch Telephone Network (PSTN). There are even cases where phone calls can be made for free, not only in a given locality but nation wide, from one state to the other, and globally.

What this means is, in the near future, phone companies will cease charging their customers for voice telephone service as everyone will be able to make a phone call from a PC. It takes only installing software that are being offered by various sources, free in some cases, and a mike and an earphone to empower a PC to do the whole job. Alternatively, it is possible to use an analog adapter by plugging a conventional telephone into it or what are known as IP phones that are directly connected to a router could also be used to avail the service. The IP phone comes with a software and the equipment is capable of making telephone calls. It is not only that VoIP is offering a very low-cost telephone service.

VoIP service had been possible because of the capability that came into existence when converting analogue into digital form was possible. The converted digital analogue could be changed into a package that could be sent through an Internet connection and it will be received by another converter at the other end that will convert it back into analogue, the final form that will reach the receiver at the other end.

The key here is both the VoIP and the traditional phones are using some sort of mechanism to transport the analogue from one point to the other, and both of them change it into a digital format, then it is sent in a big bundle with other similar calls making the procedure cost effective. In the VoIP case, what is required is a high speed Internet connection that is available through telephone lines or cable that users are paying for to have access to the Internet. However, charging for the duration both ends stayed on the line conversing was the way the telephone companies were making money. Now that has become irrelevant with one version of VoIP, when the call is between two PCs, because people can leave the service on the whole day, and can talk as many times as they want, yet it does not cost any money.

That cost also had been eliminated in some cases with conventional calling, where there are companies that provide free software to make free phone calls, and these companies make money from advertising. Those who are charging money, because they do not have any overhead, they can lower their price to a level that will make the traditional telephone companies unprofitable.

The outcome, according to some reports, has startled telephone companies, because their very existence is threatened. The number of people who are using their PC to avail a telephone service is on the rise and by the year 2006 it has surpassed five million. Still a miniscule number, yet, the number of people that are converting to VoIP is 150,000 people a day around the world, a figure for one company alone, which has more than 50 million subscribers globally, known as Skype that was recently bought by eBay for $2.6 billion dollars.

Ebay has stated that it is planning to use the company's software to enhance its auction business, where every auctioneer will have the icon of the system on their desktop and while buying and selling if there is a need to dialog, it is just a matter of clicking on the icon and the two dealers can start conversing about what they are selling and buying, with no cost at all.

Moreover, the other touted use the Skype software is supposed to deliver is that these same icons could be placed on web pages and if surfers click on them to talk, for example with a sales representative, the company will pay both companies a fee for what is dubbed as "pay-per-call". And it is going to be a copycat of what the other search engines like Google and Yahoo have made a lot of money on, the text version "pay-per-click" advertising. And major technology companies that include Microsoft, Google, Yahoo, AOL, and more have availed similar service to their customers free of charge, where users can strike conversation like a live text chat by simply clicking on a button after downloading the software each company provides to a desk top.

Even if VoIP's growth is anticipated to be phenomenal, for now it has few setbacks like for example it is not possible to access 911 or 411 service because VoIP uses IP-addressed telephone numbers, which makes it difficult to pinpoint the geographical origin of the call from the IP address of the caller. This results in making it difficult where to direct the emergency calls, however, including geographical location in the call package is in the making. Otherwise, the providers cannot continue to give service, because emergency calls are vital services that no one should go without, and the government had intervened very recently where the providers are working to comply with the requirement.

In a time of an emergency, when there is a power failure for any reason, telephone lines are always on, and could be used to make any emergency call. However, the fact that the Internet, for the most part, is still fully dependent on AC power makes it vulnerable to outages at a time of needs, even if power substitutes are available. And the vulnerable nature of the PC itself, where it is susceptible to be hacked or attacked by virus, making it inoperable frequently also puts a measurable damper on its being a better choice, because the PMST, more or less, is stable and immune from these kinds of problems.

Nevertheless, in spite of the setbacks, the two great attractions of VoIP, for the time being, remain to be price and flexibility, especially when the long distance call is tabulated, which is said to be cheap in comparison to the traditional telephone companies, that is when it is not free.

The flexibility issue enables users to take their telephones anywhere where there is a broadband connection and it is like accessing an email from anywhere there is a connection. Or having the various software available at one's disposal on a laptop will even make things better accommodating as all that is required is a mike and an earphone to plug into the laptop to receive and make phone calls, for example. If the call is from one PC to another, it is free, but charge applies if the call involves another conventional telephone.

Consequently, what all these will mean for the telephone companies is those who are dependent on voice only for their revenue will be hard hit. And some of them will have no better choice other than embracing the new technology and keep their customer base, because even if they start charging less than the conventional service, their overhead will also come down at the same time. The end result will be having some kind of business instead of losing the customer base for newcomers like Skype and many others VoIP service providers whose number could reach to 1100. On the other hand, in the future, it is possible that there will not be charge for a voice telephone call, and instead the various companies might have to bundle it with other services and this would mean a lot for everyone even if there will be some that will pay some price they can afford to.

Likewise, an external factor like competition also has a direct impact on how prices should be affixed on products and services making drawing the fine-line a daunting task, even if its effect will be felt across the board avoiding the calamities of singling out particular entities. In addition, at times, businesses will have to bear a bare minimum profit that is if they are not pushed overboard to realize loss. However, with all these factors in play they can be instrumental to bring the cost down to zero and avail a relief here and there, which is adding to the marvel of e-commerce as the would be sole redeemer in the long run.

Applying the same procedure is possible to rent where simply keeping a nimble inventory is becoming more practical, as most businesses are adopting a system where they manufacture after they received orders, which has a double payoff. Firstly, there is no need to keep a huge inventory which is known to be costly, and secondly there is not going to be a waste as there will always be someone waiting at the other end to foot the bill. The marketing and the promotion aspect of the business might not get a significant break either. But, even if being very effective on Internet advertising is not looming yet, the cost is much cheaper when compared to the other mediums. Therefore doing effective business on the Internet might not be feasible unless there is an ad campaign through the other mediums even if, eventually that is also poised to change as the technology evolves.

Hence, e-commerce is gong to be the domain of brick-and-mortars with few exception here and there where entities like e-bay, Amazon, Google, Yahoo and the like will struggle to survive and at times they might even show a favorable outcome, nevertheless, they too are grappling to have some kind of partnership with brick-and-mortars (Amazon has already partnered with Target and City Circuit) which attest to the fact that e-commerce, by and large is a sanctuary for well established businesses, who either want to do a cost-effective business with their suppliers or who are out to render a state of the art service to their existing and prospective customers while tending to their cost factors. Google and Yahoo are planning to work with print media whose has a strong brick-and-mortar base.

Then, of course, the question that pops up is how are businesses going to harness this daunting feat in such a way that it will benefit all involved parties. Those who already have shown a success rate in an already established business have everything cut and dried for them as there are technologies that will lead them by the hand to more success and prosperity, because the presumption is whatever kind of business they are in, and if it has the potential to attract buyers offline there is no reason why the same success rate will not be attained once online. Consequently, what they will have to focus on is to come up with the right kind of technology to give their customers an effective service that is to sell whatever they are specializing in. Then of course the bitsy gritty will come into play and how efficient the web site is, when it comes to satisfy the customers' need will come into play. An ad campaign both online and offline is crucial so that starting from existing customer to would be prospects will have to be lured to the web site, and of course the effectiveness of the site will take care of the rest, as clumsy web sites will definitely instigate the abandoning of carts in the middle of the spree.

Among many of the advantages that are being cited in numerous reports, having a web outlet will instantaneously make the business go global a feat that used to be accomplished by big corporations only. However, even if the global presence comes easy, not every business might be in a position to satisfy international needs, because of logistics and the time it might take to do the delivery and the particular line of business they are in. The savvy ones, who can spot the potential and know what their products commandeer could venture into setting up a web site in the particular locals, by going as far as implementing the local language, the local currency and meeting other requirements that the local legal system has laid out. What is key here is knowing what is being brought to the fore has a potential demand. Once that assessment is over and is positive, it is a matter of opening a warehouse that will store the product and take care of the delivery. Locally, most businesses use the renowned courier companies like FedEx, UPS and the like, which will do international delivery too. Even if it might be in a small scale, some electronics equipment, books, music, some apparels like clothe and furniture could all find their way into international addresses. The decision whether to be involved in international business venture depends on the nature and agenda of the particular business.

Here again we have to bring the zero cost effect into play as it is the main driving force hand-in-hand with the goal to attain full production capacity, that will necessitate to come up with cost effective methods to part with services and products that are being manufactured. So, it does not have to be inferred as if businesses are going out of their way to make an electronic trading mechanism the answer to the malice that is contributing to the sagging nature of business, which could result in a mild recession every now and then. Before the Internet, telephone and fax were more or less doing the same thing, facilitating business. Innovation means to come up and find ways of doing better business in an ongoing basis until the potential to wring out anymore profit is exhausted, and when that snag is hit the search for a better solution will undergo. For now at least for some mortar-and-bricks that point is not at all on the horizon or might not even be. Big markets like China are opening (where even the stand-alone e-bay, which could soon be infested with problems that has to do with the integrity of its sellers had a while back invested $10 billion in China) and the rush to harness them is already on. Google and Yahoo are stepping on each other the better share of the search industry.

The fact that the aggregate effort had led to the coming into existence of an entity like the Internet is an outcome of a long-term search for better solutions. In addition, for sure, businesses are out in full force to milk it. There are, however, some unanswered questions because of what bedeviled the dot-coms who were entrepreneurs who had come up with superb new ideas for business and the end result was a catastrophic bust, although a good number of them might have departed with loads of cash, especially those who have made it to the IPO level. In addition, of course, investors in whatever form they were, the majority of them did not avoid the scorch they had to suffer, while the possibility of some investors making money might not be ruled out. However, overall it was a disaster. The fallout is that the e-commerce platform is not hospitable for stand-alone start-up entrepreneurs does manifest the fact that no matter how much it was tried, making money on the Internet is not a picnic and for sure will remain a daunting challenge for some time to come and the new generation businesses showing a better result.

On the other hand, the law of economics dictates that unless a service or a product has demand, it does not have economical value, and the metric we use to measure this particular aspect might come to the rescue of the would be entrepreneurs, so that they would distinguish fancy ideas that could be deceiving by creating false impression, from those that have core value in them that will be translated into generating income. Because, the general consensus now is the stand-alone entities have no chance of surviving even if they spend billions of dollars like Webvan.com did a while back, which is said to have spent billions of dollars in establishing warehouses and had to exit e-commerce for failing to realize profit due to sagging demand. If some of that money had been averted to create brick-and-mortar outlets, they would have definitely come to the rescue. However, others like Mywebgrocer.com Albertson's and Safeway are poised to be a success story simply because they have a brick-and-mortar backup will definitely send the message home.

There might not be anything terrible, especially in a period, when going it alone is becoming the alternative to attaining freedom in the modern world, and functionality in the recently attained technological marvel will be shortchanged, maybe because of failing to play by the rule But it does not mean that there are not businesses that are doing just great to whoever is their inceptor, although it could be at a very small scale, when compared to those that have real world outlets. What is under the limelight was their profitability to investors who want to make quick money by hopping from one business to the other. Those big shots that met these requirements must have played a significant role but their sustainability had to falter over time because they were not well grounded, which illuminates their stand-alone nature. Based on that analysis, there is still ample room and opportunity for entrepreneurs who would come up with new feasible ideas, but they will suffer a fallout when they try to grow big rapidly, which could lead to their gaining attention and when they fail to meet expectation they will be dismissed as busts.

Therefore, while established businesses are eyeing the Internet to give them what they want, which is a second outlet and the capability to bring down their cost to zero so that, a none-stop stimulating of the economy, as well as realizing a sustainable profit would be practical. The discouraged and the dismissed entrepreneurs will have to continue to probe the Internet for possibilities and should shun the drive for an overnight success if possible, because it had been proven to take them down fast if it is not attainable.

Summary

A concerted Internet marketing effort is required for both standalone businesses on the Internet and for those that want to have a Web presence for brick-and-mortar businesses, and the method they follow is similar in spite of what they are particularly doing. The obvious reason behind a marketing campaign is to drive enough traffic to the web site so that whatever the site is promoting would get buyers or customers. Online business is different from offline business, because it is heavily dependent on marketing. Once an offline business opens shop at a good location, it is possible to do business without incurring anymore expense for marketing, yet the rent paid for such good location could be prohibitive in most cases, especially when it is compared with an online business, which could be very cheap. An online business needs a vigorous marketing plan and if there is something good about it is the available Internet marketing methods could be tailor-made according to the resources of those who are running the business.

Among the many kinds of Internet marketing methods there are two major ones that most online businesses are using. The first one is generic marketing and the second one is paid advertising. Since the whole idea is to bring buyers to a site, the organic marketing offers an elaborate but affordable method of driving traffic to a web site. However, paid advertising is a shortcut when compared to organic marketing, which is known to take a long time, whereas once the cost of the advertising is paid, paid advertising will immediately go to work and it is possible to see traffic coming to the site by the hour.

Organic Marketing

Organic marketing is heavily dependent on search engines to bring traffic to a site and to accomplish that the web site will have to go through a lot of preparation. The owner of the web site could do the job or it is possible to pay money to professionals that can prepare the web site to become search engine friendly. Such measure will result in meeting the requirements of the search engines that are responsible to index web sites that are either submitted to them or that are uploaded to the Internet. To index a site and to include it into the search results, the search engines have a lot of requirement they are looking for and this process of preparing a web site for the search engine robots is known as search engine optimization (SEO), and the professionals involved in this field are known as SEOs or SEO experts. Their job is to study search engine requirements, especially the major ones like Google, Yahoo, MSN, AOL, etc.

Because of the number of web sites that are in the millions, it will be difficult for search engines to give every web site preferential treatment whenever search is conducted by surfers and put them in the first ten list of the search results, the spot every business online wants to be in. Searchers will do business with anyone that comes first on the list and has what they are looking for. It is possible that if they do not get what they want from those that are in the first ten list they might go to the second, third, etc page, but it is proven that any site that is ranked above the 100 search results cannot do business, even that could be a big number of sites to go through for most searchers that are time-strapped and want to find what they are looking for quickly. The problem here is how are search engines going to distinguish from the millions of sites they have indexed which ones will have to be in the first three pages of the search result. That is why they come up with the requirements and those that meet these requirements will get the top spot because the spiders they send out to index the sites are programmed to look for these requirements while indexing, which means sites that do not meet the requirement might not be indexed, and they are under no obligation to index every site.

The requirements differ form one search engine to the other, however, everyone pays attention to the requirements of the most frequently used search engine which is Google, and it has a good number of requirements that have to be in place, first to be indexed, because that itself could take a long time, then after being indexed to get a good position on the search results. The first most important requirement is the web site will have to be robot friendly, which means when the robots visit the web site they should be able to find what they are looking for as easily and as quickly as possible, otherwise what they will put out will be a jargon. That is one of the major works the SEOs are capable of accomplishing and those who do not want to pay can do it by orienting themselves with what is required, because there are enough guides on the Internet that teach how to optimize a web site. The key requirements here are the web site has to have a title in the title tag, what the site is doing should be explained, and there are keywords to select the site will have to be found with.

The keywords could get tricky and they are important since it is when those keywords match with what searchers are putting in the search box the sites will come out in the search result. If there are no keywords selected carefully, the site might not show up in the search result, at least not at a favorable rank, but as long as they are indexed they will be there somewhere. This is a primary step to make a web site search engine friendly and when searchers encounter the text ad, it will tell them exactly what is involved and what the site is doing.

The second important requirement search engines are looking for are links, both incoming and outgoing links. This is the most tedious work that takes time and most web site owners will either buy the list, or there are software that will do the job easily, or give the job out for services that will utilize many methods and make sure that the site is well linked with other sites. If the webmasters have time it is possible to do it and what it requires is to contact other web sites that are, more or less, doing similar things, although not exactly the same things and ask them if they want to link with the particular web site, and most web sites are willing to do so, because the tedious job of finding a link will be done for them. These incoming links will have to have quality and this quality is judged by a ranking method Google is using for example, and the ranking is from 1 – 10, 10 being the highest rank and any site that is linked reciprocally with sites that are ranked

10th will get a favorable treatment from Google, especially. And this rank is attained by how well linked a site is, which means if a site has a big number of quality links it will mean that it has an authority in what it is doing and very few sites get the 10th rank.

The other important thing search engines like Google are looking for is content, which means a bare bone site that tries to market what it is doing only does not get a good rank. In order to get a good rank there will have to be a lot of material on the web site that will give value for the visitors, and the material will have to be kept fresh, otherwise the ranking will decline. The material has to have relevance to what the site is doing and it is preferred to be in a form of an article, tutorial, newsletter, and the list could go on. One of the advantages of having fresh content on the site, at least weekly, is whenever there is a fresh content posted on the site the robot will come out to visit if it is programmed to do so through what is known as Google Map. Even if it is not programmed it will come out at least once a month to do indexing and to check on the already indexed sites and if it finds a fresh content on the site, that web site will be marked as active on its log and that will mean it will continue to be among the sites that will come out at the top when search is conducted. This way the robot can tell which sites are inactive so that they will not clutter the search results. There are many sources that can avail free material or the webmaster might have to write the material, but here one thing to take notice of is there is what is termed as duplicated material, which means if the material is available on many sites and if the robot finds out, the rank of that site could plummet, which means, as much as possible, the material will have to be original and unique.

As long as these major requirements are in place any web site has a good chance of being found for the keywords it has chosen and at the same time putting the important keywords into the title and the text makes it easy for the search engines, and it should be taken into consideration. However, if there are setbacks with this method, the first one is it takes time to be indexed and placed into the list, and that is how the system works even if there are ways to get around this problem. One of them is to start a blog using the blogs offered by the particular search engines; blogger.com belongs to Google for example, and simply starting a blog had been proven to speed up the inclusion process. After the inclusion, since a blog is very busy, it could bring out the robots on a daily basis and any site linked to the blog has a good chance of staying active and fresh continuously. The main job of SEOs is to get around the problem of not being indexed and included in the search results, and they put what is required on the site as quickly as possible and would submit the site, where doing the correct things would reduce the time it takes for inclusion in the search results.

There is also what is known as algorithm the search engines like Google are using and they change it frequently so that their system will not be manipulated and because of that the rank of a site could always change, it could even be dropped out the list for violating some of the rules the search engines introduce on an ongoing basis. Consequently, it consumes too much time or if there is a need to hire someone it could get expensive because of the needed up-keeping, and even after meeting all the requirements the uncertainty could always be there.

Paid Advertising

Paid advertising is a very fast and, more or less, a reliable way of marketing, and the most popular one is pay-per-click. Many search engines offer such advertising where customers will register for the program and the process is very simple. The Google AdWords, for example, is among the most effective, maybe affordable, and reliable advertising vehicle, and all it takes is to register with the program. The only requirement is to have a credit card, where paying up-front is not required. The keys here again are the keywords where there are different payment rates earmarked for them and to start out a customer is asked how much he or she could afford to pay for each keyword chosen. There is a daily maximum where the system will stop the advertising from running when it reaches that daily maximum. In order for the keywords to become active they have to mach the going rate and that rate will always go up and down, which requires monitoring. Once that requirements are met the ad will be up and running within the hour.

The other thing that is involved here is bidding, which could make an otherwise affordable advertising method very expensive. Bidding became necessary because of the difficulty of ranking the advertisers that could be in the thousands and all of them could pay for a given keyword. There is no method to give any of the advertisers a first rank in the search result, unless they are willing to bid for it. The process is simple and if one advertiser is willing to pay $1 for a given keyword, whenever that keyword is used by searchers and if there is no one paying that much that particular customer will get the top spot. The customer will not pay for the impressions, where the charge is .25 per 1000, and the customer pays the $1 per click through rate if someone clicks through that ad to visit the Web site, whether the customer buys or not also does not matter. What this means is if there are 100 click throughs that day the customer will pay $100, but if the customer had a maximum spending limit of $50, the ad will stop showing automatically when the total amount reaches there. Next time if another customer pays $1.01 that customer will lose the top spot and will have to pay $1.02 to get it back or to keep the top spot. It is possible to keep the top spot always by keeping the bidding amount open and if someone pays $2.00 and that is the maximum paid that customer will be charged $2.01 to get the top spot and if the highest amount of the bid is .50 that customer pays .51 whether the bid is open or not.

Since there are a big number of businesses doing similar things, when the bidding heats up some search engines show how much the highest bid is so that the customers will bid out each other, which they do for the most part, because for not getting that top spot they could lose business for a competitor. Therefore, it is difficult to judge whether the bidding is good or not, but for the most part it is affordable, and the only time it gets expensive is when similar businesses compete with each other. When compared with the organic method, many people choose the paid advertising, because it is a sure way to advertise for customers and as long as the bidding war is subdued, it is possible to at least be among the ads that show on the first page. Since it is possible to control the ad it will not run amuck and cost the customer more than the allocated budget for the advertising campaign.

More or less, these are the most effective way of advertising, even if there are other methods where banners are in use too, for example. Some businesses run affiliate programs where there are those who are willing to put a banner ad for them on their site and whenever someone clicks through the ads, and close a sale they would pay a certain percentage of the sale for the site owner. Yet, banner advertising is becoming a lukewarm advertising method, but if it is done the right way the ad could be displayed on thousands of sites and the chance of driving traffic to the site depends on how popular the other sites are.

Another popular way of advertising is email marketing where it is possible to buy email list. This list could be made up of those who have agreed to receive ads or those who sell the list will harvest them from the Internet and such ads are what are labeled as spam, could be reported, and could cause a lot of problem with internet service providers. It is possible to lose the service and suffer cancellation for sending out a big number of unsolicited emails. However, as long as any email message has the opt-out clause in the message, even if a customer asks the discontinuation of the particular messages, it is not illegal, except that when such instruction is received it should be acted upon immediately, and it is such failures that will categorize an email ad campaign as a spam. Mostly such email marketing is generated by a software that could be purchased for an affordable price and it can email out millions of ads in a short period of time and when such email arrives at the destination, almost always it will be labeled as junk mail and will be kept aside from the current and regular emails, where it can be deleted by a click of a button showing that it is not a huge problem, but it could be an effective marketing if it is administered properly.

There are other sites that can put any kind of advertising on their web site and they charge money for it and if such sites have a big traffic it is possible to get traffic from them. The ad could be in a form of a rotating banner, a rotating button, or a text ad and the amount they charge depends on the popularity of the site. It is also possible to send articles on related subjects to what are called ezines where many people go to read informative articles and it is possible to put a link back to the original site, but it might require some good reasons to attract visitor to the site.

Blog had become indispensable for anyone that is doing business on the Internet because it is possible to have a direct access to customers where interacting and getting feedback in real time is possible. It is also possible to put information about the company on the blog to be commented on, on an ongoing basis, and many businesses have found that blogging is important to promote a business or a brand.

There are indexes and malls where some of them are free and some of them charge a fee for inclusion in their list, which is not expensive for the most part and it is worth to be included in their list. Since some of them are popular they have a big number of visitors, that includes some that are free of charge, and it is possible to get traffic from them. Here, also it is possible to use an offline promotion method where it is possible to put ads on newspapers, magazines, radio, TV, flyers, even billboards could do wonder for a successful, stand-alone internet business, let alone the ones that have brick-and-mortar outlets.

It is also possible to start a newsletter where attracting opt-in customers is possible and once they start receiving the newsletter on a weekly or monthly basis, they will become good candidates for ad campaign. The fact that they have signed to receive the newsletter would mean they are interested on the business and eventually converting them into buying customers is there.

It does not matter what a business is doing, because each one of them has a different customer base that will use the Internet to do various things and the trick is to capture their attention. Nothing can be done on the Internet without having an effective web site, with few exceptions, which means whatever advertising method applied will have to be able to communicate with the visitors. What this means is after going through all the trouble, when the customers arrive at the site if the site is not well maintained, or if it is unnecessarily difficult to navigate through, customer will return back to the search results to look for a better organized site. Here the copy will have to be taken into consideration, because it is the copy that will tell the customers what is available for sale, what they get out of it, the solution part, and why should they do business with the particular web site while many others are offering similar products and services. This means the customers will have to be made to make the decision to stay and examine the site further in the first 30 seconds and that will require to have a knack in grabbing their attention, and that is the job of copywriters that are part of a marketing campaign. Web developers are also important because a professionally made web site could do the selling itself, but problems start when the landing page is too cluttered and one way out from this problem is to create as many pages as needed by making the landing page navigable.

This is an important issue because it does not make sense to spend money on marketing and when customers arrive at the site, because of not doing things properly it is possible to turn off visitors. It would affect the confidence of customers that are ready to spend money when they see things are not being done properly, and they could think that they could be in to be duped. One other advantage of doing business on the Internet is it is not expensive and it depends on the nature of the business. Those that are dealing with digital products that are downloadable from the Internet, they do not literally have a lot of expense, and they can pass that low cost to their customers. Those that are promoting and are opening another outlet for their brick-and-mortar business, the expense they incur when compared to the income they could generate, it will always remain moderate.

Consequently, as a conclusion, it is highly recommended to start out as professionally as possible. Starting from the web site design, which will cost money to have a professional site designed, the rest of the services businesses avail could make or break the business. For example there has to be a means through which buying customers will be able to pay and that aspect is no longer a problem, but if it is missing it will definitely hamstring an otherwise well to do business. Some sources encourage applying all the traditional way of marketing for an online business too, and all it takes is availing the URL wherever it is possible. On T-shirts, pens, mugs, office stationary, brochures, personal cards, all these methods are not separate from marketing a business on the Internet, the idea being to make the existence of the business known to the would be customers.

It looks like it would be easy to get customers from the Internet, because the number of visitors is high, but in reality all those customers have a big number of sites to visit and that is why it is important to get their attention somehow. It is not only that the number of businesses doing the same thing is high, which means it is only those that apply effective marketing strategy that will attract traffic and once they bring them to their site, making sure that they can make a quick decision to buy should be part of the web site itself, otherwise it will be a frustrating experience for the visitors. It will only be household name companies searchers can go directly to their web sites that can do business and the rest will remain a daunting jungle where anyone could get lost unless a deliberate effort is applied to be found.

It is also proven that none of the single marketing strategies are effective enough by themselves alone, they become effective when a good number of them are bundled together. Even if many businesses know that the paid advertising is the fastest method of doing business on the Internet, they mix it the with the organic ad campaign, because why miss out from that category. It is not only that when people search online it is difficult to tell which one they are looking at most, the search results or the paid advertising that come outside of the search results. Therefore being on both of them will avail two thronged opportunities that everyone should be looking at.

CONCLUSION

We have started out by stating exactly what it means to do business on the Internet and why people should do business online, because it is not only affordable, there is nothing to lose. They do not even have to be in business right away or ever, but what they are doing online could also be a hobby. Not to miss out from this tide all it takes is to have a web presence. To do that there has to be some means of accessing the WWW and doing it through various means is possible. Some can access the Internet from work, they might belong to a club that offers free access to its members, or the best way out is to have an Internet service provider (ISP). The price has come down so low and to find out what that means go to www.netzero.com or Google by using "affordable ISPs" and there will be dozens of them. They charge a miniscule monthly fee for giving unlimited access to the WWW, which is a 24/7 arrangement as long as they are paid. There are as well those that charge by the hour and there is not much money saved in such an arrangement compared to what the unlimited service avails.

Next comes the web site that could cost money if there is a need to make it look professional, which is the recommendation, but it is not the only possibility. There are good looking templates that could be downloaded free and all they need is tweaking them up for whatever purpose they are needed and they can be uploaded to the space most ISPs provide free. There are some services that charge money but those that are starting out will not need them unless they really know their stuff well. To make things simple there are sites like Yahoo and many others that will provide free space, free email address, free templates to choose from, or a wizard that creates web sites that are tailor made to the exact need of the webmasters.

What this demonstrates is getting started online is not at all expensive, but it might be time consuming at the beginning. Spending one weekend for getting started is not going to create any inconvenience on anyone's lifestyle or if it is a business, the initial effort will be worth it for the most part. Things will start to get complicated because simply creating a web site and uploading it to the space provided free or for a price is not enough for the most part, but it could also be enough even if the performance of the web site will be lackluster.

Therefore, that is what all this book is talking about, starting from how to create an effective web site to how to make that web site an effective tool to avail a profitable business, and it is not easy except that with the right amount of time and effort it is doable for the most part, whereas it could remain unprofitable for some. Like it was stated earlier all web sites should not be created having in mind doing a successful business, but the focus here is just happened to be that. It does not matter for whatever reason if someone wants to do business on the Internet, there are certain procedures to follow and these procedures are scattered all over the place. This book has tried to put them in one place so that it will save would be online entrepreneurs time by showing them where to look, yet it is not possible to put all the things involved in here, simply because it is vast and it evolves. So many new things could have been introduced from the time this book was started, but it has the basics and the rest is up to the would be webmasters that will have to hop from place to place to find what they exactly need to do an effective business.

Hence, it is the belief of anyone who puts such material together in a form of a book that those who come across it will find material that will lead them to other better material, because putting all the material the webmaster would enjoy finding and doing for themselves will be bulky to print, to read, to learn from, and to enjoy finally. Therefore, this publication would avail most of what new startups will need on their first or repeated online venture.

www.ingramcontent.com/pod-product-compliance
Lightning Source LLC
Chambersburg PA
CBHW051245050326
40689CB00007B/1079